Selections from
HISTORY TODAY

1730

General Editor
C. M. D. CROWDER

POLITICS
AND PERSONALITY
1760-1827

A Selection of Articles from *History Today*
with an original introductory essay by

M. J. BARNES

OLIVER & BOYD

EDINBURGH

LONDON

OLIVER AND BOYD LTD

Tweeddale Court
Edinburgh 1

39A Welbeck Street
London W 1

First published 1967

© 1967 (except as specified on pp. 25, 51, 69, 86, 104, 118)
M. J. Barnes

Printed in Great Britain by
T. and A. Constable Ltd.
Edinburgh

PREFACE

For this collection I have chosen six essays from the first
fifteen volumes of *History Today*, each centring on an
important figure from British political life in the two
generations before the first Reform Act. The choice was
wide and of excellent quality, and I am only sorry that
space did not permit me to include more. Two of the
essays—those on Pitt and Canning—have been reprinted
before in the *History Today* volume, *British Prime
Ministers* (1954), but as this has been out of print for
some considerable time I felt that the value of the essays
to the present collection fully justified a measure of
duplication. Sir Lewis Namier's "George III" has also
been reprinted before, and is included in his volume
Crossroads of Power: but the importance of the subject
and the distinction of the author made the strongest case
for its inclusion here, particularly since it is an essay
excellently suited to introduce the general reader to the
work of the historian who has had more influence than
any other on modern eighteenth-century studies. I
should like to add my particular thanks to Professor
Christie for his kindness in allowing me to include his
essay on Fox, which he plans to reprint in a collection of
his own.

PREFACE

In my introduction, I have considered the impact of personality in terms which have a general relevance to the other essays, and have used the politicians they discuss as examples where appropriate. I have attempted to avoid any duplication of material, but have used footnotes to indicate some of the points of contact where they may be useful to the reader: all the essays, of course, were originally designed to stand alone and I have not attempted to impose a unity on them, nor to synthesise their differences of argument and approach. Thanks to the generous quota of plates allowed me by the publishers, I have been able to give particular attention to the illustrations, all of which I have chosen from contemporary political cartoons: in my text I refer to them by numbers in square brackets, and a full list is given at the end of the volume. For the bulk of my information on prints, I am happy to acknowledge my great debt to the work of Mrs Dorothy George, whose volumes of the British Museum *Catalogue of Satires* represent a scholastic achievement of the highest distinction. Thanks are also due to the Trustees of the British Museum, who provided the illustrations.

From the very beginning of my work on this book, the guidance and encouragement of the General Editor, Dr C. M. D. Crowder, have been of the greatest help. I am also grateful to Professor Michael Roberts, who kindly read my manuscript and offered useful advice. Any errors or imperfections, however, must be debited to my account.

M. J. BARNES

CONTENTS

I	M. J. Barnes	Personality in Politics, 1760-1827	1
II	Sir Lewis Namier	King George III: A Study in Personality	25
III	George Rudé	Wilkes and Liberty	51
IV	Ian R. Christie	Charles James Fox	69
V	Esmond Wright	Henry Dundas: "Harry the Ninth"	86
VI	R. J. White	The Younger Pitt: The Great Solitary	104
VII	M. G. Brock	George Canning	118
		Notes on Illustration	132
		Select Bibliography	136

M. J. Barnes

PERSONALITY IN POLITICS
1760-1827

The raw material of history is man, and the study of individual men must always be an attractive and illuminating way to approach an understanding of the past. And if every historian must be aware, in the words of Richard Pares, that "history is the product of thousands of different wills, none wholly dependent upon any other", it is inevitable, none the less, when he comes to study these men individually, that he will pay more attention to those we call—without, necessarily, any moral connotation—the great men. It is true, of course, that most modern historians would give short shrift to the view of history, once popular, as a conscious and deliberate creation of some few men of destiny: indeed, there has been a clear modern tendency, owing much to the influence of Sir Lewis Namier, to emphasise that great events do not necessarily have great causes, and that men, whether "great" or not, do not necessarily understand the implications of their actions for their own time, and still less for their posterity. Yet even if we abandon the heroic mould, even if we accept Namier's Freudian view that "man's actions are mostly conditioned by factors other than reason", the men we most wish to know about remain those who appear, in their own time or since, to have had the most influence, whether that influence was reasoned or not.

The period discussed in this volume appears to be particularly rich in such great figures, and the six men studied here were unquestionably ranked among them by their own contemporaries, whether in terms of fame, or, more particularly in the case of Wilkes, of notoriety: Fox and Pitt, indeed, were commonly acclaimed as the greatest men of the age. And greatness could survive the grave. If the stature and consequence of Dundas seemed rapidly to decline once many of the special conditions he had thrived on passed away, Fox and Pitt remained giant public figures whose principles and achievements seemed, well into the Victorian age, to have a contemporary as well as a historical significance: historians, indeed, were apt to write about them with the partisan feeling normally reserved for living politicians. This extended life, however, would now appear also to be over. If Dundas has for long been a remote, unremarked figure high on his column in St Andrew Square, Edinburgh, Fox too, appropriately planted in Bloomsbury on the good Whig soil of his aristocratic Russell friends, would now seem to be as finally imprisoned in history as the Roman senators whose toga he wears. In modern Britain, for all its evolutionary constitution and love for the trappings of tradition, the life of political heroes, and villains, is as short as in Ireland it is long. Even in the national crisis of

PERSONALITY IN POLITICS

the last war, a natural time for a country to invoke the spirit of its ancient heroes, the attempt of a film about Pitt to recreate the obviously appropriate inspiration of "the pilot that weathered the storm", failed not only because it was a bad film, but because it was attempting to appeal to a myth that no longer carried force: it was not this film but an equally bad one about Nelson that Sir Winston Churchill saw again and again, and it was at least reasonable for him to hope that in others, too, it might prove a spur to patriotic effort. Nelson and Wellington, however palely, remain public figures in a way that their purely political contemporaries do not. Public houses bearing today the name of Lord Nelson hardly need a picture on their inn-signs, while the picture, indeed, could stand without the name. The Victorians also gave public houses the name of George Canning, at a time when he was remembered still as a patriotic hero and founder of a living tradition: the name survives on the inn-signs, but only as a name, signifying very little. In the United States, men from this period such as Washington, Jefferson, and Jackson remain not only as historical heroes, but great figures still accorded a contemporary significance; men to attract meaningful, almost obligatory, reference in both national and party terms. In Britain, no such myths retain validity. Legal memory was once supposed to go back to Richard I: political memory, even among the politicians themselves, would now seem to go back no further than Palmerston at most, and even he, when he is mentioned, is normally used as a convenient symbol for a world now assumed to be totally passed away.

Thus detached, the modern historian and his reader should be the better able to study the period objectively. The Whig view of the eighteenth century, so scathingly attacked by Namier and others as biassed, bad and wrong, derived essentially from a consciousness, however distorted, of a tradition living on. C. Matheson, writing his *Henry Dundas* in 1933, could, on the other hand, lament the fact that the valuable lessons which he felt could be derived from studying Dundas had, since 1914, ceased to have application, while Namier himself, approaching the period at about the same time, could the more powerfully ask for it to be treated as history, because it was history. However, even if Namier was able to achieve complete objectivity in his classic analysis of an undeniably archaic constitution—and Professor Butterfield would question even this—the stuff of politics and the politicians themselves have a more direct, and perhaps partly subjective attraction. Contrasted with the period immediately before, political issues such as the American and French Revolutions have, even in a purely British context, an appeal that is immediately modern, and so too have the politicians. Men like Wilkes, Fox, Pitt, and Canning can still touch responses which Walpole, Carteret, and the Pelhams cannot, and their greater accessibility to the modern understanding is paralleled, in a broader context, by the obviously greater popularity today of Jane Austen, Sheridan, and the Romantic poets as against Fielding, Congreve, and the Augustans. To enjoy this appeal is not to betray the purpose of history. Indeed, our sympathy can be an aid to understanding. But we must still, as Namier demands,

PERSONALITY IN POLITICS

attempt to see these men in their own context.[1] Given hindsight, we can understand how Fox came to be regarded as the first liberal: in his own time, we must understand that he was also the last great Whig.

The politics of this period are notably dominated by great personalities, and something of the public impact that they made, and the interest which they aroused, is still vividly and attractively apparent in contemporary cartoons. It is true, of course, that personality could be termed a stock-in-trade of the cartoonist at almost any time, and there is nothing intrinsically peculiar about politics viewed in personal terms, but in this period it comes to be much more strongly, and significantly, marked than before. To an important extent, this is the result of a notable development in technique, roughly coinciding, as Mrs George suggests,[2] with the emergence of Gillray and Rowlandson about 1780 and the beginning of what was to be a golden age of caricature. Hogarth had been able to give brilliant expression to a vitriolic view of Wilkes's person and personality in 1763 [1]: but Hogarth is an exception in a period marked, even at its best, by stiff, formal compositions, and of lay figures scarcely distinguishable one from another and needing all the properties, emblems, or outright labels the artist can provide to make it clear who they are meant to be. Compared with the life, vigour, and immediate impact of Gillray and Rowlandson, this style seems to belong to the seventeenth century. As a

[1] Sir Lewis Namier, "King George III: A Study in Personality", pp. 25-50.

[2] M. D. George, *Catalogue V*, xii. See Bibliography p. 140.

beginner still searching for an individual style, Gillray can show the influence of the older manner at its best [3], but he soon abandoned it. Characteristic of the change that occurred is the treatment of Fox.[3] The fox's head, which had been a simple, conventional and, in its allusion to slyness, perhaps apt symbol for the young Charles James as for his father [2], gives way to the man himself, and even the tiny figure drawn by Rowlandson in 1784 [5] is immediately recognisable without any reference to the name of the cartoon or the political event it describes. True, Gillray continues to use conventions in his treatment of personality, but they normally spring from the personality itself instead of being simply applied for purposes of recognition. Thus, the almost invariable appearance of Dundas in tartan [7, 9, 11, 13] is surely less for identification than for emphasis on his leading characteristic, a running joke perhaps all the funnier for repetition. Thus, too, in Grenville's "broad bottom" [14], Gillray neatly, and for a long time, invariably, combines supposed personal with political attributes.

Yet it is surely more than a matter of technique alone. For one thing it could certainly be said that the artists had magnificent models: even a less richly gifted cartoonist like Sayers can make a most effective Fox [4], and even a poor one can make him savagely recognisable [8]. Certainly, in the physical contrast between Pitt and Fox, so easily and aptly made characteristic of their personal and political difference, the cartoonists had targets as inviting and open to exploitation as the squinting Wilkes

[3] *Loc. cit.*

PERSONALITY IN POLITICS

who, as he himself had written, was "an incomparable subject for a print".

Even the development of costume may have helped: the smallness and the eventual disappearance of wigs gave greater emphasis to individual differences, and Canning's baldness came to be as effective a distinguishing mark as Fox's unruly mop had been. But also important is the public which the cartoonists had to appeal to, if they were to sell their prints. And it is clear that they were able to presume not only on a strong interest in public personalities, but on considerable information about them.

Though often crude in manner and point, cartoons could frequently contain more sophisticated allusions: if they could frequently yield up their meaning with little or no study, they could also contain matter presupposing careful scrutiny. If Gillray's picture of Dundas as an Indian potentate [7] would have made good sense to anyone with the relatively small political awareness needed to understand his command of Indian patronage, it also contained an allusion to a speech which Dundas had made five years before against Fox's India Bill, making a neat point on inconsistency for those who noticed and understood. Similarly, though more obviously, among the words which Fox is eating in the cartoon of 1788 [8] is Dunning's famous motion of 1780.[4] The print-shop windows provided one of the free sights of London, but, although those particularly anxious to publicise a cause could sell them at cut prices, a good cartoon might cost perhaps three shillings, and therefore

[4] See Note on Illustration, p. 132, no. 4.

aimed at buyers of some substance, while, it may be imagined, only the respectable were allowed to take up the offers of hiring folios of prints for the evening. For these and other reasons, it is clear that the cartoonists were aiming at a politically literate audience: that they could often succeed is perhaps most convincingly proved by the interest which many of the politicians themselves took in the way they were depicted.

If they might often be amused, they often had very good reason not to be. Personal attacks were made of a virulence which even today would be considered outrageous. The bitter personalities must obviously have catered to a public taste, and in appealing to it, the cartoonists were allowed a freedom which did not exempt the King himself. The stage was subject to a system of censorship, but cartoons, like newspapers, were not. Gillray, in tilting at the electoral influence of Treasury money [9], could, even at a time when the government seemed disposed to equate criticism with sedition, freely attack Pitt in just the way that Fielding had once attacked Walpole: but while Fielding's satirical playlets—virtually cartoons in action—had been driven from the stage by Walpole, his theme could remain freely available to later cartoonists as one of their stock subjects. When theatre audiences laughed at the character of Sir Pertinax McSycophant in Macklin's successful play of 1780, they may have been tempted to think of Scots politicians in general. But cartoonists could be far more explicit: in the same year, Gillray showed a diabolic tartan-clad Bute still influencing a simple king, more than a decade after he had ceased to do so [3]. For, as Mrs George points out,

PERSONALITY IN POLITICS

politicians did not seem disposed to take action for libel—perhaps, one might guess, because the ridicule they suffered would only have been heightened by the publicity and indignity of court proceedings—though attacks on the King, for instance, could be a great deal stronger than in No. 45.[5] The Wilkite theme of boot and petticoat government, in itself insulting, did not scruple to imply an intimate relationship between Bute and the King's mother, and this was reproduced in the prints: Gillray's rather repulsive *Sin, Death and the Devil* of 1792 was not dissimilar, showing a hag-like Queen Charlotte as Sin, suggestively defending Pitt, who, as Death, is actually wearing the King's crown. Again, the Prince and his brothers took successful action against the proprietor of *The Times* for libelling their good faith in wishing for the King's recovery in 1789, and he was imprisoned for two years: but Rowlandson had been able to make much the same point in a cartoon and get away with it.

The considerable freedom left to cartoonists does not mean that their influence was considered to be negligible. Governments and their opponents did not show the consistent interest in prints which they gave to newspapers, but they were not unaware of their propaganda value. Hogarth's *Wilkes* had appeared as a riposte to No. 17 of the *North Briton*, which had attacked him viciously as a paid lackey of the King: on the other side,

---

[5] Wilkes was committed in April 1763, as author and publisher of the *North Briton* No. 45, "a most infamous and seditious libel . . . tending to alienate the affections of the people from his majesty. . . ." See G. Rudé, "Wilkes and Liberty", pp. 51-3.

P.P.——B

numerous prints swelled the propaganda for Wilkes, illustrating the crimes and follies of government, often in a manner which would find expression today in touched-up photography. But if, as Mrs George suggests, government got the rough end of the stick more often than not before 1782, oppositions were more usual sufferers afterwards, and Fox, in particular, was subject to a stream of unending abuse which, if not always spontaneous, certainly reflected the unpopularity of almost every position he adopted. Sayers' brilliant exploitation of the India Bill [4] was widely felt to have had a particularly damaging effect on his public character, and when Pitt came to power, Sayers was rewarded with a minor office. That cartoons were believed to influence opinion is further illustrated by the young Canning's interest, eager as he was to promote support not only for government, but for his own personal cause.

Typically, he approached the best talent available—Gillray's—and was instrumental in getting a pension for him from Pitt's Government, with the result that, even if Gillray's ironic genius could not be relied on for continuously unambiguous support, Pitt as the cunning Treasury manipulator of 1796 had become Pitt as *Integrity Retiring* from the Treasury in 1801. Canning suggested subjects for cartoons, and planned to ally Gillray's genius with his own writing talent in the Pittite publicity of the *Anti-Jacobin*: that he had personal influence over Gillray is shown by his intervention in the series *French Habits*, when Canning, who had no objection to Fox's being shown as a member of the

PERSONALITY IN POLITICS

French Directory [12], asked Gillray to withdraw a similar picture of Sheridan, and was obliged.

The ambitious Canning was also particularly keen for personal publicity, and clearly hoped that Gillray would help to launch him as a public figure. He was impatient for his debut, as Wilkes once had been in 1762: disappointed that it did not happen as quickly as he wished, he clearly felt it better to be attacked than ignored. And when he did appear, kissing the toe of the great Pitt in *The Giant Factotum* [11], his appearance was notably contrived and artificial: the meticulous Gillray was forced to use the clumsy device of sticking a paper bearing the name Canning into the pocket of the little figure who would otherwise have meant little or nothing to the public. In spite of the absurdity of the position, however, Canning may well have been flattered at the implication, even if Gillray makes it quite clear that while Canning is doing the kissing, Dundas is doing the supporting. Canning's consequence soon grew but, as Mrs George points out, Gillray continued to exaggerate it and give it greater prominence than in the other cartoons. *Confederated-Coalition* [13] of 1804 can surely be taken as notably partial—not surprisingly, since, in showing the arrayed talents attacking Addington, it represented the aim dearest to Canning's heart at the time, even if the style of the print may not have been all he could have desired: Canning, though small, is in a position suggesting the role he coveted as Pitt's chief lieutenant, while he is drawn with a line noticeably less harsh, so that, among the grotesques, Gillray makes him appear a miniature hero. Later still, towards the end of his career,

Gillray gave expression to the great dream of Canning's political life [14]: as Pitt-Elijah ascends to Heaven, he drops his mantle to the Pittites below at the Altar of the Constitution, and it is clear that the mantle is to fall first to Canning as the new prophet, who looks up with confidence to receive it. It may be added that it was to be nearly twenty years before he did receive it—and then in somewhat torn condition—and by then Canning had long given up chasing fame so overtly. The flood of cartoons that acclaimed his appointment as premier in 1827 [15] reflected a more genuine popularity.

If cartoonists, as has been said, turn naturally to personalities, there still seems to be a significant emphasis in this period on politics cynically pictured as a struggle simply of personal ambition, or worse; a matter of men, not measures. Thus, if Fox is castigated again and again for his French principles in the 1790s, it is made abundantly clear that their chief attraction for him is as a means of gaining power [12]. Gillray is particularly jaundiced in this way, and his *Confederated-Coalition* [13] is one of his most withering and elaborate treatments of the theme. Here, under Jupiter's eagle (George III), the Addingtonians try to ward off the opposition giants below who are striving to displace them in the Heaven of the Treasury, while Tierney, the renegade Foxite, encourages other renegade reinforcements to ascend behind the scenes. If cynical, the cartoon is also well informed, and the leading attackers, the Pittites and the Fox-Grenvilles, are shown in a concurrent, but not united, assault—a correct reflexion of their attitude in the Commons. But if the giants have no clothes, they do not

PERSONALITY IN POLITICS

seem either to be encumbered with principles or policies. Fox is drawn, for once, without reference to any one of his unpopular principles, and his French banner has been left to Burdett on the side-lines: Pitt, clad in bits of a commander-in-chief's apparel, is about to hurl not policies but "knock-down arguments", and at his feet the *coup de grâce* lies ready. In the words of the Miltonic inscription, their aim is "not to destroy, but root them out of heaven", and there is little enough evidence that anything but a change of personnel is intended. The Grenvilles were reported to be pleased with the print, though they were claiming—and with success—to be acting in the national interest. But George III might well have liked it, too: he would have seen what he felt he saw in reality in 1804, the ambition of faction.

At the beginning of his reign, George III had not been alone in thinking that government had become the prize of faction, sought by selfish groups of men in Parliament who were held together by family ties and personal ambitions that seemed to subordinate the national interest. Wilkes, biassed perhaps by his own disappointed hopes of preferment, cast a similarly cold eye on the professed principles of party politics when he said that every Whig, on attaining office, became a Tory: he also felt, and the charge had wide appeal, that the King himself had been guilty, in championing Bute, of subordinating the national to the personal. If this was partly true, it was from inexperience chiefly, and the King never made quite that mistake again: if his personal attachments and dislikes remained strong, he could claim reasonably, if naïvely, that they were based on national considerations. Throughout his life, his ideal remained a government of, and supported by, all good men and true, high above party and faction. It was a dream shared by many independent M.P.s, and it was paid lip-service, and sometimes more, by the professional politicians themselves. And, even if the Chatham experiment failed, George III could still feel that with North the dream might be made reality. At just this time, however, in the cause of the greatest remaining family group, the Rockinghams, Burke produced his eloquent defence of party as a body of men agreed on great principles, serving public not private ends, and defended it as a development to be prized, not abhorred. Like Fox and Canning later, Burke dismissed the anti-party slogan, "measures not men", as cant; but at least his emphasis on principle as a bond promised that measures and men might go together.

In the 1770s, Burke's views had some chance of early fulfilment. The great issues of the American War period made it possible to divide the Commons for motives that could reasonably be termed national, even if it was hardly principle that enlisted Fox in the Rockingham ranks[6]: public interest in the War and the Wilkite victory of 1771,[7] which effectively established the freedom of newspapers to report speeches in the Commons, helped to emphasise that party debate was national debate. And when, in 1782, a body of independents warned North that they could no longer support him, and thus forced his resignation, the Rockinghams seemed

[6] Ian R. Christie, "Charles James Fox", pp. 76-7.
[7] G. Rudé, pp. 64-5.

PERSONALITY IN POLITICS

to have made their point. If a hostile cartoon could show them chaining up the King [2], at least Rockingham himself was shown disposing of the Crown "for the Publick Use".

Yet faction was soon to seem stronger than ever. If there was an obvious smack of personal rancour and rivalry in Fox's break with Shelburne, his ensuing union with North seemed outrageously factious. Against Fox, Pitt strove successfully to show himself the scourge of faction, and the champion of the nation's interest.[8] By the 1790s, with a broad and weighty coalition now including many ex-Foxites who felt they were giving up party to serve the nation in its crisis, and supported by the King and by overwhelming numbers in the Commons and outside, Pitt, though his power was capable of more than one view [10], seemed to be providing the kind of government that George III and so many independents had wanted: while, on the other side, Foxites, now reduced to a small band that could have no hope of office, represented far more of an adhesion to disinterested party principle than could ever be possible in their more numerous and more heterogeneous troops of the 1780s. Yet, on Pitt's resignation in 1801, George III must soon have felt that chaos was come again, while, in an anarchy of groups and individuals, Burke's theories seemed less applicable than ever. The groupings, re-groupings, ruptures, and reconciliations of the period up to 1812 made it a period of one long barter: the bargains that were struck were surprising enough, but for every one made another two or three were discussed, and no

[8] R. J. White, "The Younger Pitt: The Great Solitary", pp. 109-10.

combination seemed too astonishing to contemplate. Old enemies became friends, then enemies again: past differences of policy and principle, however bitter, were readily forgiven and forgotten, with scant attention paid to how identified they were likely to be in the future. It was indeed a period for the politics of personality, a period when personal huffs and slights could assume the greatest importance, when the way in which an approach was made could count for more in the decision than the content of the approach itself: the language of negotiation and explanation was singularly dignified, but it was a language in which honourable conduct was more often mentioned than agreed policies. Fox returned to his old love of coalitions with the ex-Pittite Grenville, a man who disagreed with a good half of his principles: Fox was delighted with his open and manly conduct, Grenville no less delighted with Fox's nobility which, in 1804, redoubled his determination not to join Pitt's government without him. Some Foxites of the 1790s, however, were less impressed by this honeymoon. Pitt himself found it a good deal less easy, in spite of his Olympian explanations, to appear as disinterested out of office as he had been in it: George III resented his behaviour and spoke of faction. Of course, like the others, Pitt had easily convinced himself that personal ambition and national good were one, as all politicians must do: but he went furthest of all.[9] In a letter to Melville (Dundas) he could state as a simple axiom requiring no comment that he could serve the nation as Prime Minister only, and nothing less. He compelled the King, moreover,

[9] *Op. cit.* p. 107, for a sympathetic treatment of Pitt's ambition.

1. 1763. "... done as like as I could as to feature at the same time some indication of his mind ..." wrote Hogarth, who took sketches during Wilkes's trial in Westminster Hall.

2. 1782. George III is chained up by the new Rockingham ministry. At his feet are Fox and (?) Lord John Cavendish:

Burke, Conway, Keppel, and Richmond are standing, while Rockingham himself takes away the crown.

3. 1780. Sandwich, Germaine, and North botch their work while George III looks on admiringly with a devilish Bute at his shoulder.

PERSONALITY IN POLITICS

with some personal asperity, to agree to exclude Addington, who was, for the King in 1804, the very epitome of a good man and true. If Pitt's manners were more polite, his method was not far from Foxite. Canning was no more ambitious than Pitt had been throughout his life—that was impossible—but even in such a period he could make himself a bad name for intrigue,[10] though he was at least unlucky that his quarrel with Castlereagh became the most sensational of the period by ending in a duel.

Yet again, the same process recurred after 1812: Liverpool's character and persistence managed to hold together some notably hostile temperaments, and to rebuild a Pittite governing party of wide appeal that included most of the political talent available. Canning formally disbanded his little personal group in 1814 and shortly afterwards joined the Cabinet. In the Grenvilles, the last of the great family groups was absorbed, and they returned to their spiritual and material home to leave the Whigs once more a basically Foxite party, while the re-emergence of the name Tory on the government side, even if it covered a wide range of opinion and interest, served to emphasise the national validity of party difference. Once more, with Liverpool's retirement, the façade collapsed. If Wellington and Peel had good reasons of principle for refusing to serve under Canning in 1827, they allowed them to be sufficiently disguised to enable both George IV and the country at large to think them factious and personal, and Canning was able to flatter the King by reminding him that he could now refuse to bow to Tory faction as his father had refused

[10] M. G. Brock, "George Canning", p. 119.

the Whigs [15]. Many Whigs joined Canning, but Grey remained aloof to rage with Wellington, and he could hardly have put his reasons in more insultingly personal terms.[11]

Sir Keith Feiling speaks of the personal hatred of Wellington for Canning as producing the end of a party: much the same could be said of Fox's vendetta with Shelburne, and even of Pitt's personal misunderstandings first with Addington, then with Grenville. Yet if personality could be disruptive, it could also be cohesive. Not only was the machinery of party discipline in its infancy, but principles as a binding force could not stretch beyond the very general: it was an empirical age, and measures were mostly treated on their merits as the need arose. In such a situation, party groupings were bound to admit of many questions on which colleagues could agree to differ, and the loyalty that certain men could inspire became an important kind of political cement. That loyalty might be based on electoral influence, as in the case of Dundas and his train of Scots,[12] but it could also derive from the personality of certain great men. Hence the currency, in this period, of the names Foxites, Pittites, and Canningites as descriptive political labels.

Of all politicians, Fox was the most personal in the attitudes he adopted and attracted.[13] When Burke formally announced the end of his political friendship with Fox, he showed some consistency with his own

[11] *Op. cit.*, p. 121.

[12] Esmond Wright, "Henry Dundas: 'Harry the Ninth'", pp. 92-6.

[13] I. Christie, pp. 72, 76, 78.

PERSONALITY IN POLITICS

definition of party principle: Fox, as he made clear in one of the most emotional scenes the Commons ever witnessed, could not understand why completely opposite views of the French Revolution should break their long-standing personal bond. And when the Portlands joined Pitt for similar reasons, Portland for more than a year seemed totally incapable of making the decision, so great was the personal grief it cost him to break with Fox. Fox's personality, indeed, remained by far the most important magnetising agent in his party, able to hold on to old supporters however bleak the prospects, and however tempting the offers of government, able even to enlist new ones when the natural tendency of any bright young man would be to hitch his fortunes to the government—though, it should be added, Canning had been able to resist the charm for something of that reason.

Far less obviously sociable and charming than Fox, Pitt proved capable of attracting little less than the same worship. If one was "Charles", or at least "Fox", and the other, even to the older Dundas, could still be "Mr Pitt", the effect was similar. Already, in early 1784, Dundas was writing to his children that "my attachment to Mr Pitt personally grows more and more unbounded every day, and of course to fight by his side ... gives me more heartfelt pleasure than I ever enjoyed since I was in Parliament". Dundas never thought of himself as a party man, but his deep attachment to Pitt lasted to the grave and had much the same effect. "I could not admire or love him more", Canning wrote in 1796, and when, in 1803, he voted differently from his leader for the first time in his life, he expressed dramatic regrets. From the first, Canning had set himself to achieve a more informal relationship with Pitt than was usual, and, as he proudly wrote, he succeeded. He became, as Malmesbury noted, a son to Pitt—albeit, as he added, a spoiled one.

The loyalties inspired by Fox and Pitt helped to give a sense of party and of a party continuity which survived not only the re-alignments of groups, but also their own deaths. Foxites might vary in number, they might join with new allies or lose old friends, but they still retained their identity as Foxites. After his death, Pitt's heirs differed among themselves, and did not necessarily adhere to his policies: yet Perceval, Liverpool, Castlereagh, and Canning could rightly feel themselves following the spirit of the master. The kind of inspiration these men evoked and bequeathed is aptly portrayed in Gillray's cartoon [14], though most unkindly to Fox. It owed much to the accident of their careers: Fox was almost always in opposition, Pitt in government. Thus, Pitt left behind a governing tradition, with followers, like himself, totally convinced that they were the natural rulers, and confident of their ability to rule. Fox, who, in spite of his occasional storming efforts, never had the drive of Pitt's ambition, and who, even in office, never gave the impression of wanting to stay there long, left to his followers the habit of opposition, and the spirit to stand almost unending exclusion: perhaps, indeed, even to enjoy it. The charm that idleness had for him, and the somewhat lackadaisical attitude to power of his later years, seemed to infect not only Grey, his heir apparent, but

PERSONALITY IN POLITICS   21

even the once Pittite, once place-hungry Grenville. Early in his career, Fox wrote that he was willing to forego power, but still wished to acquire great reputation: Pitt, late in life, wrote that above power he prized the reputation of great character.[14] Their followers, well into the nineteenth century, were certain that they had achieved their aims.

Personal allegiances, of course, claimed only a proportion of the Commons: on the eve of Addington's fall, Foxites and Grenvilles both numbered about seventy, Pittites a dozen less, while Addington took about the same number with him when he resigned office. What had persuaded Addington to resign, however, was not simply the party numbers now arrayed against him, formidable though these were, but the waning of support from the less committed—men who, though generally well disposed to vote for any government with the King's confidence, expected a convincing case to be made by its spokesmen. Votes could not be counted automatically, they had to be won; and, in the fight for them, the floor of the House was held again and again by the same leading performers. Only a minority of the members aspired to play such a part, and the ability to play it was the essential foundation of the political eminence of Fox, Pitt, Dundas, and Canning. It was this ability which enabled Pitt to stand up to Fox in 1783 and after, and thus justify George III's choice: had it not been for Pitt, Fox might well have been able to make himself indispensable to any government, and certainly, on Pitt's death,

---

[14] Canning offered a slight variation on the theme: "My road", he wrote in 1801, "must be through *character* to power".

George III quietly accepted the man he had rejected with contumely only two years before. It was this ability which forced George IV, more sulkily, to accept that Canning was the only possible successor to Castlereagh in 1822. But it was more than debating ability which made succeeding generations look back on this period as an age of giants.

Sourly surveying the Commons in 1834, Greville wrote that Peel was the best orator in a poor field, but, though good, "he is at an immense distance below the great models of eloquence, Pitt, Fox, and Canning". It had been an age which prized oratory for its own sake, and, conscious of the greatness of its heroes, had often compared them with the giants of classical antiquity. As in so many other ways, manner and style attracted particular attention: thus, one observer noted that a speech of Dundas's had been "more close in argument as well as more correct in language and composition" than usual, while many others commented on particular qualities of voice or delivery in this or that speaker. It is true that speeches could be praised for style rather than content: Fox and Pitt frequently expressed their admiration for each other's efforts, without necessarily agreeing with a word that had been said. But in such subjects as the American Revolution, Warren Hastings, and the French wars, and in the recurrent theme of the constitution itself, the great speakers had matter worthy of their powers, giving them an interest far greater than their art alone provided. And they could the better take these opportunities for majestic orations because of the relatively light claim of detailed, technical business on the

PERSONALITY IN POLITICS

members' time, and their tolerance in allowing speeches to range far beyond the immediate matter in hand.

Nor was the effect of these speeches confined any longer to the members and the lucky few able to compete for places in the public gallery. The wide, if imperfect, publication of debates helped to ensure that the great figures of the Commons would also be the great figures of the nation. Many speakers themselves took an interest in correcting their speeches for publication, while, as Professor Aspinall remarks, the space given by the newspapers to Parliamentary proceedings is vivid testimony of a public interest almost unthinkable today. The political nation was broadening at an unprecedented rate, while the basis of the Commons remained narrow and unreformed. But yet, partly at least by this publicity, the House remained the great political cockpit of the kingdom. When Canning produced his famous words, "I called the New World into existence to redress the balance of the Old", a friend noted that the words acted like electricity on the members "who all rose for a moment to look at him". But, as Canning well knew, it was an electricity which would be felt through the length and breadth of the nation.

Many of the techniques employed by modern historians concentrate increasing attention on the study of men in economic or social groups, but the importance and interest of individual personality continues to be emphasised by students of the politics of this period. Biographical studies, for instance, have recently appeared on previously neglected figures such as Addington and Perceval, Sir Francis Dashwood and Samuel Whitbread:

the publication of the first volumes of the *History of Parliament* has offered succinct biographies of every member who sat in the Commons between 1754 and 1790. And while lesser figures are studied perhaps for the first time, the greater men continue to be re-assessed: thus, further full biographies are in preparation on Fox, Pitt, and Canning. The documentary evidence of the period is rich and far from exhausted, and Professor Rudé's work on the impact of Wilkes's career may be taken as but one example of the way that information can be gathered from sources previously little used. But it is not only the advance of knowledge which requires the re-writing of history. Each generation, it is often said, has its own ways of looking at the past, while even in an agreed framework of historical method there is still great scope for difference. Modern attempts to see the eighteenth century on its own terms may be paralleled with the move to play eighteenth-century music as it was written, and not as in Victorian arrangements: but, just as there can be no definitive version of the *Messiah*, so no interpretation of George III and the Rockinghams is likely to find unanimous acceptance. History is a debate, and there can be no better justification for a volume of essays written by different historians.

Sir Lewis Namier

KING GEORGE III
A Study in Personality [1]

There were three large pictures of George III at the
exhibition of Royal Portraits arranged by the Academy
of Arts in the Spring of 1953. Looking at the first, by
Reynolds, painted when the King was 41, I was struck
by the immaturity of expression. The second, by Law-
rence, painted in 1792 at the age of 54, depicts him in
Garter robes; face and posture seem to attempt in a
naïve, ineffective, and almost engaging manner to live
up to a grandeur which the sitter feels incumbent on him.
The third, by Stroehling, painted in November 1807,
at the age of nearly 70, shows a sad old man, looking
dimly at a world in which he has no pleasure, and which
he soon will not be able to see or comprehend.

A picture in a different medium, of the King and his
story, presents itself to the student when in the Royal
Archives at Windsor he surveys the papers of George

---

[1] Copyright © Sir Lewis Namier. Royal Academy of Arts lecture,
27 May 1953. Published in *History Today*, III (1953), pp. 610-21, and
in Namier: *Crossroads of Power*, London (Hamish Hamilton) 1962.

P.P.—C

III. They stand on the shelves in boxes, each marked on a white label with the year or years which it covers. The eye runs over that array, and crucial dates recall events: 1760, '65 and '67, '74 and '75, '82 and '83, 1789, '93, '96, 1802, 1805—the series breaks off in 1810; and brown-backed volumes follow, unlabelled: they contain the medical reports on a man shut off from time, which means the world and its life.

Fate had made George III ruler when kings were still expected to govern; and his active reign covered half a century during which the American conflict posed the problem of Imperial relations, while at home political practice constantly ran up against the contradiction inherent in the then much belauded "mixed form of government": personal monarchy served by Ministers whose tenure of office was contested in Parliament. Neither the Imperial nor the constitutional problem could have been solved in the terms in which the over-whelming majority of the politically-minded public in this country considered them at the time: but George III has been blamed ever since for not having thought of Dominion status and parliamentary government when constitutional theory and the facts of the situation as yet admitted of neither.

In the catalogue, *Kings and Queens*, on sale at the exhibition, the introduction dealing with the reign of George III gave the traditional view of his reign:

> Conscientious and ambitious, he tried to restore the political influence of the Crown, but his intervention ended with the humiliating American War of Independence.

KING GEORGE III

Conscientious he certainly was, painstakingly, almost painfully, conscientious. But was he ambitious? Did he try to exercise powers which his predecessors had relinquished, or claim an influence which was not universally conceded to him? And was it the assertion of Royal, and not of Parliamentary, authority over America which brought on the conflict and disrupted the First British Empire?

Let us place ourselves in March 1782. Dismal, humiliating failure has turned public opinion, and the House of Commons is resolved to cut losses and abandon the struggle; it is all over; Lord North's government has fallen; and the King is contemplating abdication. He has drafted a message to Parliament (which was never sent); here are its first two paragraphs:

> His Majesty during the twenty-one years he has sate on the throne of Great Britain, has had no object so much at heart as the maintenance of the British Constitution, of which the difficulties he has at times met with from his scrupulous attachment to the rights of Parliament are sufficient proofs.
>
> His Majesty is convinced that the sudden change of sentiments of one branch of the legislature has totally incapacitated him from either conducting the war with effect, or from obtaining any peace but on conditions which would prove destructive to the commerce as well as essential rights of the British nation.[2]

In the first paragraph the King declares his unswerving devotion to the British Constitution, and shows himself conscious of his difficulties in America having arisen through "his scrupulous attachment to the rights of

---

[2] Fortescue, *Correspondence of King George III*, vol. V, no. 3061.

SIR LEWIS NAMIER

Parliament"; the second paragraph pointedly refers to the Commons as "one branch of the legislature", and gives the King's view of the American war: he is defending there the vital interests and essential rights of the British nation.

A year later, in March 1783, when faced by the necessity of accepting a Government formed by the Fox-North coalition, George III once more contemplated abdication; and in a letter (which again was never sent) he wrote to the Prince of Wales:

> The situation of the times are such that I must, if I attempt to carry on the business of the nation, give up every political principle on which I have acted, which I should think very unjustifiable, as I have always attempted to act agreable to my duty; and must form a Ministry from among men who know I cannot trust them and therefore who will not accept office without making me a kind of slave; this undoubtedly is a cruel dilemma, and leaves me but one step to take without the destruction of my principles and honour; the resigning my Crown, my dear Son to you, quitting this my native country for ever and returning to the dominions of my forefathers.
>
> Your difficulties will not be the same. You have never been in a situation to form any political system, therefore, are open to addopt what the times may make necessary; and no set of men can ever have offended you or made it impossible for you to employ them.[3]

Alongside this consider the following passage from a letter which George III wrote on 29 Dec. 1783, after having dismissed the Coalition and while he was trying

[3] Windsor MSS.

KING GEORGE III

to rally support for the newly-formed Administration of the younger Pitt:

> The times are of the most serious nature, the political struggle is not as formerly between two factions for power; but it is no less than whether a desperate faction shall not reduce the Sovereign to a mere tool in its hands: though I have too much principle ever to infringe the rights of others, yet that must ever equaly prevent my submitting to the Executive power being in any other hands, than where the Constitution has placed it. I therefore must call on the assistance of every honest man . . . to support Government on the present most critical occasion.[4]

Note in these two passages the King's honest conviction that he has always attempted to do his duty; that he has been mindful not to infringe the rights of others: but that it would be equally wrong in him to submit "to the Executive power being in any other hands, than where the Constitution has placed it". And while I do not for a moment suggest that these things could not have been done in a happier manner, I contend that the King's statements quoted above are substantially correct.

In the eighteenth century, a proper balance between King, Lords, and Commons, that is, the monarchical, aristocratic and representative elements of the Constitution acting as checks on each other, was supposed to safeguard the property and privileges, the lives and liberty of the subjects. Single-chamber government would have been no less abhorrent to that century than royal autocracy. The executive was the King's as truly as it is now

[4] Windsor MS. 5709.

of the President in the United States; he, too, had to choose his Ministers: but from among Parliamentary leaders. And while aspirants to office swore by the "independency" of the Crown and disclaimed all wish to force themselves on the King, if left out they did their level best to embarrass and upset their successful rivals. The technique of Parliamentary opposition was fully established long before its most essential aim, which is to force a change of government, was recognised as legitimate; and because that aim could not be avowed in its innocent purity, deadly dangers threatening the Constitution, nay the life of the country, had to be alleged for justification. Robert Walpole as "sole Minister" was accused of arrogating to himself the powers of both King and Parliament; the very tame Pelhams, of keeping George II "in fetters"; Bute, who bore the name of Stuart, of "raising the standard of Royal prerogative"; and George III of ruling not through the Ministers of his own choice whom he avowed in public, but through a hidden gang of obscure and sinister "King's friends". It is obviously impossible here to trace the origin and growth of that story, or to disprove it by establishing the true facts of the transactions to which it has become attached—it was a figment so beautifully elaborated by Burke's fertile imagination that the Rockinghams themselves finished by believing it, and it grew into an obsession with them. In reality the constitutional practice of George III differed little from that of George I and George II. William Wyndham was proscribed by the first two Georges as a dangerous Jacobite, and C. J. Fox by the third as a dangerous Jacobin; while the elder Pitt

KING GEORGE III

was long kept out by both George II and George III on personal grounds. But for some the Royal veto and Royal influence in politics lose their sting if exercised in favour of successful monopolists in Whiggery.

I go one step further: in the eighteenth century the King had to intervene in politics and was bound to exercise his political influence, for the party system, which is the basis of Parliamentary government, did not exist.[5] Of the House of Commons itself probably less than half thought and acted in party terms. About one-third of the House consisted of Members who looked to the King for guidance and for permanency of employment: epigoni of earlier courts or forerunners of the modern civil service; and if they thus pursued their own interest, there is no reason to treat them as more corrupt than if they had done so by attaching themselves to a group of politicians. Another one-fifth of the House consisted of independent country gentlemen, ready to support the King's Government so long as this was compatible with their conscience, but averse to tying themselves up with political groups: they did not desire office, honours, or profits, but prided themselves on the disinterested and independent line they were pursuing; and they rightly claimed to be the authentic voice of the nation. In the centre of the arena stood the politicians, their orators and leaders fighting for the highest prizes of Parliamentary life. They alone could supply the façade of governments: the front benches in Parliament. But to achieve stability a Government required the active support of the crown and the

[5] For a fuller discussion of this point see my Romanes Lecture, *Monarchy and the Party System* (1952).

32   SIR LEWIS NAMIER

good opinion of the country. On matters about which public opinion felt strongly, its will would prevail: but with the House constituted as it was, with the electoral structure of the unreformed Parliament, and an electorate which neither thought nor voted on party lines, it is idle to assume that modern Parliamentary government was possible.

I pass to the next point: was George III correct in saying that it was "his scrupulous attachment to the rights of Parliament" which caused him the difficulties in America? Undoubtedly yes. It was not Royal claims that the Americans objected to, but the claims of "subjects in one part of the King's dominions to be sovereigns over their fellow-subjects in another part of his dominions".[6] "The sovereignty of the Crown I understand", wrote Benjamin Franklin; "the sovereignty of Britain I do not understand. . . . We have the same King, but not the same legislature". Had George III aspired to independent royal power nothing could have suited him better than to be sovereign in America, the West Indies, and possibly in Ireland, independent of the British Parliament; and the foremost champions of the rights of Parliament, recalling the way in which the Stuarts had played off Ireland and Scotland against England, would have been the first to protest. But in fact, it would be difficult to imagine a King simultaneously exercising in several independent countries executive powers in conjunction with Parliamentary leaders. It will suffice to remember the difficulties and jealousies which Hanover caused although itself

[6] Benjamin Franklin to the Rev Samuel Cooper of Boston, 8 Jun. 1770.

KING GEORGE III

politically inert. The two problems which George III is unjustly accused of having mismanaged, those of imperial and constitutional relations, were inter-connected: only after responsible government had arisen did dominion status within the Commonwealth become possible. Lastly, of the measures which brought on the American conflict none was of the King's making: neither George Grenville's Stamp Act, nor the Declaratory Act of the Rockinghams, nor the Townshend Duties. All that can be said against him is that once the struggle had started he, completely identifying himself with this country, obstinately persevered in it. He wrote on 14 Nov. 1778:

> If Lord North can see with the same degree of enthusiasm I do, the beauty, excellence, and perfection of the British Constitution as by law established, and consider that if any one branch of the Empire is alowed to cast off its dependency, that the others will infalably follow the example . . . he . . . will resolve with vigour to meet every obstacle . . . or the State will be ruined.[7]

And again on 11 Jun. 1779, expecting that the West Indies and Ireland would follow:

> Then this island would be reduced to itself, and soon would be a poor island indeed.[8]

On 7 Mar. 1780:

> I can never suppose this country so far lost to all ideas of self importance as to be willing to grant America independence, if that could ever be universally adopted, I shall despair of this country being ever preserved from

[7] Fortescue IV, no. 2451.

[8] *Ibid.*, no. 2649.

a state of inferiority and consequently falling into a very low class among the European States . . .[9]

And on 26 Sep. 1780:

> . . . giving up the game would be total ruin, a small State may certainly subsist, but a great one mouldering cannot get into an inferior situation but must be annihilated.[10]

When all was over Lord North wrote to the King on 18 Mar. 1782:

> Your Majesty is well apprized that, in this country, the Prince on the Throne, cannot, with prudence, oppose the deliberate resolution of the House of Commons: . . . Your Majesty has graciously and steadily supported the servants you approve, as long as they could be supported: Your Majesty has firmly and resolutely maintained what appeared to you essential to the welfare and dignity of this country, as long as this country itself thought proper to maintain it. The Parliament have altered their sentiments, and as their sentiments whether just or erroneous, must ultimately prevail, Your Majesty . . . can lose no honour if you yield at length . . .
>
> Your Majesty's goodness encourages me . . . to submit whether it will not be for Your Majesty's welfare, and even glory, to sacrifice, at this moment, former opinions, displeasures and apprehensions (though never so well-founded) to . . . the public safety.[11]

The King replied:

> I could not but be hurt at your letter of last night. Every man must be the sole judge of his feelings, there-

[9] Fortescue V, no. 2963.
[10] *Ibid.*, no. 3155.
[11] *Ibid.*, no. 3566.

KING GEORGE III

fore whatever you or any man can say on that subject
has no avail with me.[12]

What George III had never learnt was to give in with
grace: but this was at the most a defect of character.

II

Lord Waldegrave, who had been Governor to the
Prince of Wales 1752-6, wrote in 1758 a character sketch
of him so penetrating and just that it deserves quoting
almost in full.[13]

> The Prince of Wales is entering into his 21st year,
> and it would be unfair to decide upon his character in
> the early stages of life, when there is so much time for
> improvement.

A wise preamble: yet a long and eventful life was to
change him very little. Every feature singled out by
Waldegrave finds copious illustration in the 50 years that
followed (in one case in a superficially inverted form).

> His parts, though not excellent, will be found very
> tolerable, if ever they are properly exercised.
>
> He is strictly honest, but wants that frank and open
> behaviour which makes honesty appear amiable. . . .
>
> His religion is free from all hypocrisy, but is not of the
> most charitable sort; he has rather too much attention to
> the sins of his neighbour.
>
> He has spirit, but not of the active kind; and does not
> want resolution, but it is mixed with too much
> obstinacy.
>
> He has great command of his passions, and will
> seldom do wrong, except when he mistakes wrong for

---

[12] *Ibid.*, no. 3567.
[13] James, 2nd Earl Waldegrave, *Memoirs* (1821), pp. 8-10.

right; but as often as this shall happen, it will be difficult to undeceive him, because he is uncommonly indolent, and has strong prejudices.

His want of application and aversion to business would be far less dangerous, was he eager in the pursuit of pleasure; for the transition from pleasure to business is both shorter and easier than from a state of total inaction.

He has a kind of unhappiness in his temper, which, if it be not conquered before it has taken too deep a root, will be a source of frequent anxiety. Whenever he is displeased, his anger does not break out with heat and violence; but he becomes sullen and silent, and retires to his closet; not to compose his mind by study or contemplation, but merely to indulge the melancholy enjoyment of his own ill humor. Even when the fit is ended, unfavorable symptoms very frequently return, which indicate that on certain occasions his Royal Highness has too correct a memory.

Waldegrave's own endeavour was to give the Prince "true notions of common things".[14] But these he never acquired: which is perhaps the deepest cause of his tragedy.

The defect Waldegrave dwells upon most is the Prince's "uncommon indolence", his "want of application and aversion to business". This is borne out by other evidence, best of all by the Prince's own letters to Bute:[15]

[14] James, 2nd Earl Waldegrave, *Memoirs* (1821), p. 64.

[15] See *Letters from George III to Lord Bute* (1939), edited by Romney Sedgwick, from which all such letters are quoted. Mr Sedgwick's edition is a masterpiece of scholarship. To mention but one aspect: from internal evidence he has succeeded in dating some 330 undated letters.

KING GEORGE III

July 1st, 1756: I will throw off that indolence which if I don't soon get the better of will be my ruin.

March 25th, 1757: I am conscious of my own indolence ... I do here in the most solemn manner declare, that I will throw aside this my greatest enemy ...

September 25th, 1758: ... that incomprehensible indolence, inattention and heedlessness that reigns within me ...

And he says of his good resolutions: "as many as I have made I have regularly broke": but adds a new one: "I mean to attempt to regain the many years I have fruitlessly spent".

December 19th, 1758: ... through the negligence, if not the wickedness of those around me in my earlier days, and since perhaps through my own indolence of temper, I have not that degree of knowledge and experience in business, one of my age might reasonably have acquir'd ...

March 1760: ... my natural indolence ... has been encreas'd by a kind of indifference to the world, owing to the number of bad characters I daily see ...

By shifting the blame on to others, he tries to relieve the bitter consciousness of failure: which is one source of that excessive "attention to the sins of his neighbour" mentioned by Waldegrave. Indeed, George III's letters, both before and after his accession, are full of it: "the great depravity of the age", "the wickedest age that ever was seen", "a degenerate age", "probity and every other virtue absorb'd into vice, and dissipation"; &c. "An ungrateful, wicked people" and individual statesmen alike receive castigation (*in absentiâ*) from this very young Old Testament prophet. Pitt is "the blackest of hearts", "the most dishonourable of men", and plays "an infamous and ungrateful part"; Lord Temple, an "ungrateful, arrogant and self-sufficient man"; Charles Townshend is "a man void of every quality", "the worst man that lives", "vermin"; Henry Fox, a man of "bad character", "void of principles"; Lord Mansfield is "but half a man"; the Duke of Bedford's character "contains nothing but passion and absurdity"; &c. As for George II, the Prince felt ashamed of being his grandson. And on 23 Apr. 1760, half a year before his accession, aged 22, he wrote to Bute: " . . . as to honesty, I have already lived long enough to know you are the only man who possesses that quality . . ."

In Bute he thought he had found the tutelary spirit who would enable him to live up to his future high vocation. Here are further excerpts from the Prince's letters to him:

> *July* 1*st*, 1756: My friend is . . . attack'd in the most cruel and horrid manner . . . because he is my friend . . . and because he is a friend to the bless'd liberties of his country and not to arbitrary notions . . .
>
> By . . . your friendship . . . I have reap'd great advantage, but not the improvement I should if I had follow'd your advice . . .
>
> I will exactly follow your advice, without which I shall inevitably sink.
>
> *March* 25*th*, 1757: I am resolved . . . to act the man in everything, to repeat whatever I am to say with spirit and not blushing and afraid as I have hitherto . . . my conduct shall convince you that I am mortified at what I have done and that I despise myself . . . I hope this will

KING GEORGE III

persuade you not to leave me when all is at stake, when nobody but you can stear me through this difficult, though glorious path.

In June 1757 Leicester House were alarmed by rumours of an alliance between the Duke of Newcastle and Henry Fox, and were ascribing fantastic schemes to the Duke of Cumberland. The Prince already saw himself compelled to meet force by force or to "yield up the Crown",

> for I would only accept it with the hopes of restoring my much loved country to her antient state of liberty; of seeing her ... again famous for being the residence of true piety and virtue, I say if these hopes were lost, I should with an eye of pleasure look on retiring to some uninhabited cavern as this would prevent me from seeing the sufferings of my countrymen, and the total destruction of this Monarchy ...
>
> *August 20th*, 1758: ... by ... attempting with vigour to restore religion and virtue when I mount the throne this great country will probably regain her antient state of lustre.

Was this a Prince nurtured in "arbitrary notions", ambitions to make his own will prevail? or a man with a "mission", striving after naïvely visionary aims? No doubt, since early childhood it must have been rammed into him, especially when he was being reproved, to what high station he was born; and disparaging comparisons are said to have been drawn between him and his younger brother. He grew up with a painful consciousness of his inadequacy: "though I act wrong perhaps in most things", he wrote on one occasion. Excessive demands on a child, complete with wholesome exhortations, are fit to reduce it to a state of hebetude from which it is not easy to recover. A great deal of the pattern of George III's behaviour throughout life can be traced back to his up-bringing.

He spent his young years cut off from intercourse with boys of his own age, till he himself ceased to desire it. Bubb Dodington notes in his *Diary* on 15 Oct. 1752, that the Princess Dowager of Wales

> did not observe the Prince to take very particularly to anybody about him, but to his brother Edward, and she was glad of it, for the young people of quality were so ill-educated and so vicious, that they frightened her.

And so they did him for the rest of his life. Isolation by itself would be apt to suggest to a child that there was something wrong with those he had to shun: but this he was probably told in so many words. On 18 Dec. 1753, Dodington records another talk with the Princess:

> I said, it was to be wished he could have more company. She seemed averse to the young people, from the excessive bad education they had, and from the bad examples they gave.

So the boys spent joyless years in a well-regulated nursery, the nearest approach to a concentration camp: lonely but never alone, constantly watched and discussed, never safe from the wisdom and goodness of the grown-ups; never with anyone on terms of equality, exalted yet oppressed by deferential adults. The silent, sullen anger noted by Waldegrave was natural to one who could not hit back or speak freely his mind, as a child would among children: he could merely retire, and nurture his griefs and grievances—and this again he continued through life.

4. 1783. Fox makes off with the India House and its patronage. "Fox said that *Sayers's caricatures* had done him more mischief than the debates in Parliament or the works of the press", wrote Lord Eldon.

5. 1784. Britannia disposing of Fox and North.

KING GEORGE III

On 3 May 1766 during a political crisis, he wrote to Bute: "I can neither eat nor sleep, nothing pleases me but musing on my cruel situation." Nor could he, always with adults, develop self-reliance: at 19 he dreamt of reforming the nation, but his idea of acting the man was to repeat without blushing or fear what he had to say.

For the pious works which were "to make this great nation happy" Bute's "sagacious councils" were therefore indispensable. When in December 1758 Bute expressed doubts whether he should take office in the future reign, the Prince in a panic searched his own conscience:

> Perhaps it is the fear you have I shall not speak firmly enough to my Ministers, or that I shall be stagger'd if they say anything unexpected; as to the former I can with great certainty assure that they, nor no one else shall see a want of steadiness either in my manner of acting or speaking, and as to the latter, I may give fifty sorts of puts off, till I have with you thoroughly consider'd what part will be proper to be taken . . .

George III adhered to this programme. On his grandfather's death he waited to hear from Bute what "must be done". When expecting Pitt at a critical juncture: "I would wish to know what I had best say. . . ." With regard to measures or appointments: "I have put that off till I hear my Dear Friend's opinion"; "If this [is] agreable to my D. Friend I will order it to day . . ."; "I desire my D. Friend to consider what I have here wrote, if he is of a contrary opinion, I will with pleasure embrace it." And when in November 1762 Bute declared he would retire on conclusion of peace:

SIR LEWIS NAMIER

> I had flattered myself [wrote the King] when peace
> was once established that my D. Friend would have
> assisted me in purging out corruption . . . ; . . . now . . .
> the Ministry remains compos'd of the most abandon'd
> men that ever had those offices; thus instead of re-
> formation the Ministers being vicious this country will
> grow if possible worse; let me attack the irreligious, the
> covetous &c. as much as I please, that will be of no
> effect . . . Ministers being of that stamp . . .

Two years on the throne had worked little if any
change in his ideas and language; nor did the next twenty.
The same high claims on himself, and the same incapacity
to meet real situations he was faced with: hence his
continued dependence on others. By 1765 he saw that
Bute could not help him, by the summer of 1766 he had
written off Bute altogether. In the spring of 1765 he
turned to the Duke of Cumberland, the bugbear of his
young years: "Dear Uncle, the very friendly and warm
part you have taken has given me real satisfaction. . . ."[16]
And to Pitt "the blackest of hearts": "My friend for so
the part you have acted deserves of me. . . ."[17] In July
1765 Cumberland formed for him the Rockingham
Administration and presided over it a quasi-Viceroy:
but a few months later Cumberland was dead. In July
1766 Chatham formed his Administration: but a few
months later his health broke down completely. Still
George III clung to him like a mollusc (a mollusc who
never found his rock). "Under a health so broken",
wrote Chatham, "as renders at present application of

[16] Fortescue I, no. 74.
[17] *Ibid.*, no. 94.

KING GEORGE III

mind totally impossible. . . ."[18] After nearly two years of waiting for his recovery, the King still wrote: "I think I have a right to insist on your remaining in my service."[19] Next he clung to the ineffective Grafton who longed to be relieved of office; and when Grafton resigned, the King wrote to him on 27 Jan. 1770:

> My heart is so full at the thought of your retiring from your situation that I think it best not to say more as I know the expressing it would give you pain.[20]

Then came North. Totally unequal to the difficulties of the American crisis, in letter after letter he begged the King to let him resign. Thus in March 1778:

> Lord North cannot conceive what can induce His Majesty, after so many proofs of Lord North's unfitness for his situation to determine at all events to keep him at the head of the Administration, though the almost certain consequence of His Majesty's resolution will be the ruin of his affairs, and though it can not ward off for a month that arrangement which His Majesty seems to apprehend.[21]

But the King would not hear of it. 2 Jul. 1779: "no man has a right to talk of leaving me at this hour. . . ."[22] 25 Oct. 1780: he expects North "will shew that zeal for which he has been conspicuous from the hour of the Duke of Grafton's desertion".[23]

[18] *Ibid.*, no. 538.
[19] Fortescue II, no. 669.
[20] Grafton MSS.
[21] Fortescue IV, no. 2241.
[22] *Ibid.*, no. 2696.
[23] Fortescue V, no. 3165.

George III's attitude to North conformed to the regular pattern of his behaviour. So did also the way in which after a while he turned against North in bitter disappointment. By the '70s the King spoke disparagingly of Bute and Chatham; and in time his imagination enabled him to remember how on the day of his accession he had given the slip to them both. A month after Grafton had resigned, George III wrote to him: "I ... see anew that the sincere regard and friendship I have for you is properly placed...."[24] Somewhat later his resignation changed into "desertion". When North, resigned: "I ever did and ever shall look on you as a friend as well as faithful servant...."[25] But incensed at the new situation he soon started attacking North, and treated him niggardly and unfairly over his secret service accounts. George III's attachment was never deep: it was that of a drunken man to railings—mechanical rather than emotional. Egocentric and rigid, stunted in feelings, unable to adjust himself to events, flustered by sudden change, he could meet situations in a negative manner only, clinging to men and measures with disastrous obstinacy. But he himself mistook that defensive apparatus for courage, drive, and vigour, from which it was as far removed as anything could be. Of his own mental processes he sometimes gave discerning though embellished accounts. Thus to Bute in 1762: "I ... am apt to despise what I am not accustom'd to ..." And on 2 Mar. 1797, to the younger Pitt when criticising the way measures were weakened in passing through Parliament:

[24] 2 Mar. 1770, Grafton MSS.
[25] Fortescue V, no. 3593.

KING GEORGE III

My nature is quite different I never assent till I am convinced what is proposed is right, and then . . . I never allow that to be destroyed by after-thoughts which on all subjects tend to weaken never to strengthen the original proposal.[26]

In short: no after-thoughts, no reconsideration—only desperate, clinging perseverance.

Still it might be said: at least he broke through his indolence. Yes, indeed: from pathologically indolent he turned pathologically industrious—and never again could let off working: but there was little sense of values, no perspective, no detachment. There is a legend about a homunculus whose maker not knowing what to do with him bid him count poppy-seed in a bag. That George III was doing with his own busy self. His innumerable letters which he copied in his own hand, or the long documents transcribed by him (he never employed an amanuensis till his eye-sight began to fail), contain some shrewd perceptions or remarks, evidence of "very tolerable parts if . . . properly exercised". But most of his letters merely repeat approvingly what some Minister, big or small, has suggested. "Lord A. is very right . . ."; "General B. has acted very properly . . ."; "the minute of Cabinet meets with my fullest concurrence . . ."; "Nothing can more deserve my approbation than"—whatever it was. But if a basic change is suggested, his obstinacy and prejudices appear. On 15 Mar. 1778 in a letter to Lord North, he makes an unusual and startling admission:

I will only add to put before your eyes my most inmost thoughts, that no advantage to this country nor personal

[26] Windsor MSS.

46 SIR LEWIS NAMIER

danger can ever make me address myself for assistance either to Lord Chatham or any other branch of the Opposition. . . .[27]

As a rule he would sincerely assert, perhaps with somewhat excessive ostentation, that first and foremost he considered the good of the country. When told by Bute that it would be improper for him to marry Lady Sarah Lennox, he replied: "the interest of my country ever shall be my first care, my own inclinations shall ever submit to it" (and he added: "I should wish we could next summer ... get some account of the various Princesses in Germany"—and he settled down to "looking in the New Berlin Almanack for Princesses"). When considering withdrawal from the German War, he wrote (with a sidelong glance at the late King) about the superiority of his love "to this my native country over any private interest of my own. . . ." He was "a King of a free people"; "I rely on the hearts of my subjects, the only true support of the Crown", he wrote in November 1760. They will not desert him—

if they could be so ungrateful to me who love them beyond anything else in life, I should then I really believe fall into the deepest melancholy which would soon deprive me of the vexations of this life.

The same note, of love for this country and trust that his subjects would therefore stand by him, continues for almost twenty years. But gradually other overtones begin to mix with it. He had become the target of virulent attacks and unjust suspicions which he deeply resented.

[27] Fortescue IV, no. 2221.

KING GEORGE III

Thus to Lord North on 7 Mar. 1780: " . . . however I am treated I must love this country".[28] And to the Prince of Wales on 14 Aug. 1780:

> The numberless trials and constant torments I meet with in public life, must certainly affect any man, and more poignantly me, as I have no other wish but to fulfill my various duties; the experience of now twenty years has convinced me that however long it may please the Almighty to extend my days, yet I have no reason to expect any diminution of my public anxiety; where am I therefore to turn for comfort, but into the bosom of my own family?[29]

And he appealed to his son, the future George IV, to connect himself only with young men of respectable character, and by his example help "to restore this country to its former lustre",—the old tune once more. And, in another letter:

> From your childhood I have ever said that I can only try to save my country, but it must be by the co-operation of my children only that I can effect it.[30]

In the 1780s there is a more than usually heavy crop of bitter complaints about the age by one "righteous overmuch": "it has been my lot to reign in the most profligate age", "depravity of such times as we live in", "knavery and indolence perhaps I might add the timidity of the times. . . ." And then:

> I thank Heaven my morals and course of life have but little resembled those too prevalent in the present age, and certainly of all objects in this life the one I have

[28] Fortescue V, no. 2963.
[29] Windsor MSS.
[30] *Ibid.*

> most heart, is to form my children that they may be useful examples and worthy of imitation . . .[31]

With the King's disappointments in country and son another note enters into his letters. He warns the Prince—

> in other countries national pride makes the inhabitants wish to paint their Princes in the most favourable light, and consequently be silent on any indiscretion; but here most persons if not concerned in laying ungrounded blame, are ready to trumpet any speck they can find out.[32]

And he writes of the "unalterable attachment" which his Electoral subjects have shown to their Princes. When George III went mad in 1788, he wanted to go back to Hanover. Deep down there was a good deal of the Hanoverian in him.

His insanity was a form of maniac depression. The first recorded fit in March 1765 was of short duration, though there may have been a slight relapse in May; and a year later he wrote to Bute—

> if I am to continue the life of agitation I have these three years, the next year there will be a Council [of] Regency to assist in that undertaking.

During the next twenty-three years he preserved his normal personality. The attack in 1788 lasted about half a year: the King was over 50, and age rendered complete recovery more difficult. His self-control weakened and his irritability increased. He was conscious of a growing weakness. Yet there was something about him which more and more endeared him to the people. He was never popular with London society or the London mob; he was

[31] Windsor MSS.
[32] *Ibid.*

KING GEORGE III
49

much beloved in the provinces—perhaps it was his deeper kindness, his real piety, and sincere wish to do good which evoked those feelings. These appear strikingly, for instance, in his own account of his journey to Portsmouth in 1778,[33] and in Fanny Burney's account of his progress through Wiltshire in 1789.[34] He was not a politician, and certainly not a statesman. But in things which he could judge without passion or preconceived ideas, there appears basic honesty and the will to do the right thing. I shall limit myself to two examples. When in 1781 a new Provost was to be appointed at Eton, George III insisted on choosing a man "whose literary tallents might make the appointment respectable ... for Eton should not be bestowed by favour, but merit".[35] And when in 1787 a new Lord Lieutenant had to be chosen for Ireland, the King wrote to the younger Pitt about the necessity

> of looking out for the person most likely to conduct himself with temper, judgment, and an avowed resolution to avoid partiality and employ the favours he has to recommend to with the justice due to my service and to the public. ... When I have stated this Mr. Pitt must understand that I do not lean to any particular person ... when I state that a Lord Lieutenant should have no predilection but to advance the public good I should be ashamed to act in a contrary manner.[36]

I have given here a picture of George III as seen in his letters, "warts and all". What I have never been able to find is the man arrogating power to himself, the ambitious

[33] *Ibid.*
[34] Fanny Burney, *Diary* (1905), vol. IV, pp. 310-11.
[35] Fortescue V, no. 3455.
[36] Windsor MSS.

schemer out to dominate, the intriguer dealing in an underhand fashion with his Ministers; in short, any evidence for the stories circulated about him by very clever and eloquent contemporaries. He had a high, indeed an exaggerated, notion of royalty but in terms of mission and duties rather than of power; and trying to live up to this idealised concept, he made unreasonable demands on himself. Setting himself unattainable standards, he could never truly come to grips with reality: which condemned him to remain immature, permanency of inner conflict precluding growth. Aware of his own inadequacy, he turned to others and expected them to enable him to realise his visionary programme (this appears clearest in his relations with Bute); and he bitterly reproached them in his own mind, and blamed the age in which he lived, for his own inevitable failure. The tension between his notions and reality, and the resulting frustration, account to a high degree for his irritability, his deep-seated resentments, and his suppressed anger—for situations intolerable and disastrous for himself and others; and it may have been a contributory factor in his mental breakdowns. The desire to escape from that unbearable conflict repeatedly shows itself in thoughts of abdication which must not be deemed insincere because never acted upon (men of his type cannot renounce their treadmill). He himself did not understand the nature and depth of his tragedy; still less could others. There was therefore room for the growth of an injurious legend which made that heavy-burdened man a much maligned ruler; and which has long been accepted as history.

George Rudé

WILKES AND LIBERTY [1]

In the course of an eventful life and public career, John Wilkes achieved much and stirred many passions. His name is, of course, most frequently linked with the constitutional liberties which he played so conspicuous a part in wresting from an unwilling Parliament and a bitterly hostile Government. Scarcely less remarkable than the achievement itself were the means employed: the stimulation and direction of the political energies not only of City merchants and liverymen and Middlesex freeholders, but of far wider circles among those "middling and inferior set of people" whose particular champion he professed to be. It is of this latter kind that the "Wilkes and Liberty" movement, which played so striking a role in the political battles of the 1760s and 1770s, was essentially composed.

The cry "Wilkes and Liberty" was first heard at Westminster Hall in May 1763. The famous No. 45 of Wilkes's weekly journal, the *North Briton*, had appeared

[1] [Copyright © George Rudé. Originally published in *History Today*, VII (1957), pp. 571-9.]

on 23 April. The Government, eager to seize its opportunity, issued a "general warrant" for the apprehension of the writers, printers, and publishers of the offending number. Wilkes, despite his claim to immunity as a Member of Parliament, was put in the Tower. Brought before Chief Justice Pratt in the Court of Common Pleas, at Westminster Hall, on 3 May, he was greeted with shouts of "Liberty! Liberty! Wilkes for ever!" The case being adjourned, he appeared again before Pratt three days later, made a vigorous speech in his defence, and was discharged. As he left the Court to return to his house in Great George Street nearby, the rafters shook with a mighty cry of "Whigs for ever and no Jacobites" and "Wilkes and Liberty".

It was the first round in a prolonged political battle: but Wilkes's triumph was short-lived. The Government, through its spies, managed to get possession of one of a dozen copies of an obscene parody of Pope's *Essay on Man* that Wilkes had had printed on his private press for circulation among his intimates. Its reading in the House of Lords in November, though it did little good to the already tarnished reputation of the Earl of Sandwich, who read it, was more immediately damaging to Wilkes himself: his allies, including Chatham, were scandalised, and the Lords' condemnation of the *Essay on Woman* as "a most scandalous, obscene, and impious libel" followed closely on a Commons debate at the end of which it was ordered that *North Briton* No. 45 should be burned at the Royal Exchange by the Common Hangman. This, however, proved to be more easily said than done: a "great multitude" of Wilkes' supporters, "to the number

WILKES AND LIBERTY

of 500 and more", gathered on 3 December at the appointed place, pelted the Sheriffs with mud and dirt, and prevented the executioner from discharging his duty. Later, at the Old Bailey, John Franklin, a ship's steward, was fined 6s. 8d. and imprisoned in Newgate for three months for his part in the affair.

Yet, despite this display of public support, and the award, a few days later, of £1,000 damages for the illegal seizure of his papers, Wilkes decided to disappear from the political scene. When summoned to answer further charges before the House of Commons, he used the pretext of a wound incurred in a recent duel to postpone his attendance; and, on Christmas Eve, he slipped down to Dover by post-chaise, and crossed to France the next day. His enemies were not prepared to accept excuses: on 20 Jan. 1764, he was expelled from the Commons; at the end of February, he was prosecuted in his absence before Chief Justice Mansfield in the Court of King's Bench on the double charge of publishing No. 45 and printing the *Essay on Woman*; and, on 1 November, having failed to appear, he was formally pronounced an outlaw. Four years of not unpleasurable exile in Paris and Italy followed.

But Wilkes did not intend to stay permanently out of the public eye. Having failed to secure a pardon or preferment through the intervention of influential friends, he decided to return home to stake his political fortune on the General Election of 1768. He crossed to England on 5 February and challenged the authorities to take notice of his presence by addressing a letter to the King on 4 March. This remaining unanswered, he had himself admitted to the Livery of the Joiners' Guild and presented himself for election in the City of London on 16 March. He received the enthusiastic support of the small masters and craftsmen, who gave him a resounding (though unofficial) majority on a first "show of hands": but, as expected, when it came to the official poll—from which his supporters were largely excluded—he emerged bottom of the list of six candidates. Quite undaunted, he announced his intention to contest in Middlesex and, when he left the Guildhall, "the populace ... to show their zeal, took the horses from his carriage and drew it themselves".

The Middlesex election opened on 28 March. Though Wilkes lacked the solid support of influential backers, his closest associates (prominent among whom were his counsel, Serjeant Glynn, and the Rev John Horne of Brentford) did their work well: 40,000 hand-bills were distributed and every passenger in 250 coachloads of Wilkesite supporters was given a blue cockade and a "Wilkes and Liberty" card. Wilkes himself rode to the hustings at Brentford Butts, "attended by an amazing number of people". He headed the poll from the start and his election was never in doubt: but the result was not announced until late in the evening, as a recount had been called for to determine which of the two other candidates— George Cooke and Sir William Beauchamp Proctor— should have second place.

The election itself was perfectly orderly, though some attempt was made at Hyde Park Corner to prevent Wilkes's opponents from reaching Brentford. According to Horace Walpole, the Spitalfields weavers—as always

WILKES AND LIBERTY

champions of the "patriot" party—had mustered in strength in Piccadilly, giving out blue cockades and papers inscribed "No. 45, Wilkes and Liberty". A scuffle followed, as objection was raised to a flag carried by Proctor's supporters, bearing the painted words, "No blasphemer", and other unflattering epithets addressed to the popular candidate. In reporting the incident, the *Annual Register* added the curious observation:

> There has not been so great a defection of inhabitants from London and Westminster, to ten miles distant, in one day, since the lifeguardsman's prophecy of the earthquake, which was to destroy both these cities in 1750.

There had been, also, a considerable "defection" of magistrates and constables to cope with the crowds that had gathered at Brentford and its approaches; the peace officers remaining in Westminster and London were quite insufficient to cope with the riots that followed. For two days, Wilkes's supporters held the streets and noisily celebrated his victory. Citizens were obliged to light up their windows at night and every door from Temple Bar to Hyde Park was, it was said, chalked with "No. 45". The rioters, wrote the *Annual Register*,

> demolished all the windows of Lord Bute, Lord Egmont, Sir Samson Gideon, Sir William Mayne, and many other gentlemen and tradesmen in most of the public streets of both cities, London and Westminster. ... At Charing Cross, at the Duke of Northumberland's, the mob also broke a few panes; but his Grace had the address to get rid of them by ordering up lights immediately into his windows, and opening the Ship alehouse, which soon drew them on that side.

An eye-witness spoke of "a Mob of about 100 Men and Boys" setting out from Charing Cross about nine o'clock in the evening on 29 March and smashing windows in Leicester Fields, Covent Garden, Russell Street, the Strand, Long Acre, Oxford Street, and Piccadilly. Before becoming lost to view in Southampton Street, they had broken the Duke of Newcastle's windows off Lincoln's Inn Fields and the lamp over Sir John Fielding's door in Bow Street, and drunk two gallons of beer to "Wilkes and Liberty" at the *Six Cans* in Turnstile, Holborn. Among those arrested as the result of this incident was one Matthew Christian, a "gentleman of character and fortune", late of Antigua, who was alleged to have spent £6 or £7 on filling the rioters with beer in a number of ale-houses. The same evening, according to a newspaper report, there was a riot in Wood's Close, Clerkenwell:

> and while a laundress in that place was putting out lights, some of the villains went into the yard, and carried away upwards of forty ruffled shirts, the property of divers persons.

Meanwhile, some thousands had gathered, the previous night, before the Mansion House—the Lord Mayor, Thomas Harley, was a staunch Court supporter—and, to shouts of "Wilkes for ever", had broken nearly every window and lamp in the building. We learn from the Mansion House Committee's minutes that the accounts later submitted by City glaziers for the repair of the damage amounted to £174 for window-panes and £30 4s. for lighting lamps. It is, therefore, hardly surprising that

6. 1784. George III and Wilkes, who was now a supporter of Pitt, the "little Child".

7. 1788. Dundas as the ruler of India, accused of achieving what he had attacked Fox for attempting in 1783, with "One Foot in Leadenhall Street and the other in the Province of Bengal".

WILKES AND LIBERTY

the Common Council of the City, for all its Wilkite sympathies, should, at its meeting on 30 March, have resolved "to prosecute with the utmost Rigour such persons who have (been) active in the said Riots"; to pay a £50 reward "upon the conviction of each of the above offenders"; and "to prosecute with the utmost vigour all Persons who shall hereafter be guilty of any such Riots or Disorders". A lull followed during the first weeks in April, though there persisted an undercurrent of unrest in the capital (partly attributable, no doubt, to the high cost of food) that needed little pretext to bring it to the surface. Such an occasion was afforded by Wilkes's brief appearance at the Court of King's Bench, where he formally surrendered to his outlawry on 20 April. On leaving the Court, he was attended by a large crowd, though there was no immediate disturbance. The same evening, in Shadwell, however, his temporary release was celebrated by a large band of Irish coal-heavers, who had mustered to settle accounts with an unpopular coal "undertaker". Before making an armed assault on his public house in New Gravel Lane, they were heard to shout, "Wilkes and Liberty, and Coal-heavers for ever!" There were further cries of "Damn you, light up your candles for Wilkes"; and soon every house along the Ratcliff Highway was lighted up in his honour. Similar disturbances were reported from the provinces: we learn from a press account of a few days later that

> At Newcastle the cry for Wilkes and Liberty is said to be as loud among the sailors as at London, and attended with the same violence.

P.P.—E

More widespread demonstrations were touched off in London by Wilkes's appearance for trial at Westminster Hall on 27 April. Having been committed to the custody of the Marshal of the King's Bench prison, he left the Court at 6.30 in the evening in the company of "Parson" Horne of Brentford. Crowds formed in Palace Yard and along Westminster Bridge. The horses were unharnessed and the prisoner's carriage drawn in triumph along the Strand and Fleet Street to the *Three Tuns* tavern in Spitalfields. Here Wilkes appeared at an upper window and was acclaimed by his supporters, before disappearing in disguise and surrendering to his gaolers at the King's Bench prison in St George's Fields.

From then on, riots were continuous for almost a fortnight. "The next day", writes a local chronicler,

> the prison was surrounded by a prodigious number of persons, but no disturbances happened till night, when the Rails which enclosed the footway were pulled up to make a fire, and the Inhabitants of the Borough were obliged by the Mob to illuminate their houses, but a Captain Guard arriving soon after 12 the Mob dispersed.

A few days later, an attempt was made to demolish the lobby of the prison; and, on 10 May, there followed the far more violent affray known as the "Massacre of St George's Fields". It was the day of the opening of Parliament, and many of the thousands who gathered in the Fields from all over the capital seem to have done so in the hope of seeing John Wilkes escorted to Westminster. Others were there, of course, with the more pointed object of demonstrating their support for the Wilkite

WILKES AND LIBERTY

cause. Shortly before midday, some persons broke through the ranks of the Foot Guards guarding the prison and affixed to the wall a paper with the doggerel:

> Venal judges & Ministers combine
> Wilkes and English Liberty to confine;
> Yet in true English hearts secure their fame is,
> Nor are such crowded levies at St. James's.
> While thus in Prison Envy dooms their stay,
> Here, O grateful Britons, your daily homage pay,
> Philo Libertatis no. 45.

When, at the instance of the magistrates, the paper was pulled down, the demonstrators became restive: there were shouts of "Give us the paper" and "Wilkes and Liberty for ever", and stones were thrown at the soldiers. Mistaking William Allen, the son of a local publican, for one of their assailants, soldiers shot him dead in a nearby cow-house. The Riot Act was read and the Guards were ordered to fire. "Five or six", wrote the *Annual Register*, "were killed on the spot & about 15 wounded".

In revenge for the shooting, the houses of two Southwark justices, Edward Russell of Borough High Street, and Richard Capel of Bermondsey Street, were attacked and "pulled down": it was reported that "the activity of the two gentlemen ... in suppressing the tumults occasioned the outrage". According to Capel's account of the assault, after his own house had been attacked, he was called to Russell's house in the High Street, where

> one John Percival took him by the collar and said, "Damn you, I'll mark you"; and accordingly he did mark him with large figures *No. 45* on the cape of his great Coat.

60   GEORGE RUDÉ

Meanwhile, a band of 500 sawyers had "pulled down" a saw-mill in Limehouse, recently built for Charles Dingley, a prosperous City merchant; and once again, windows, lamps, and furniture had been smashed by a large crowd at the Mansion House. On this occasion, a gibbet was carried along Cornhill, bedecked with a boot and a petticoat;[2] "there were great hissing and hallooing", stated a witness, and cries of "Wilkes and Liberty".

While such lawless behaviour must have caused alarm among solid citizens, the Government's own reputation had been badly shaken by the "massacre" of St George's Fields. It was not improved by the publication in the press of a letter sent by Lord Barrington, Secretary of War, to the officer in charge of the Foot Guards, commending his men for their conduct on 10 May. The Government may have drawn comfort from the condemnation to prison of half a dozen of some twenty-five persons arrested during the disturbances of the past fortnight, but it was distinctly embarrassed by the verdict of "wilful murder" returned by the coroner's jury enquiring into the death of William Allen, and even more by the committal for trial at the Old Bailey on a similar charge of Samuel Gillam, one of the justices officiating at St George's Fields. Wilkes himself, though duly sentenced on 18 June to a fine of £1,000 and to twenty-two months' imprisonment for his various misdemeanours, was not slow to take advantage of the Government's follies; and, a few weeks later, he was able to publish in the *St James' Chronicle*, with suitable com-

---

[2] This was the current Opposition symbol for Lord Bute and the King's mother, the Princess Dowager.

WILKES AND LIBERTY

ments, the instructions sent by Lord Weymouth, Secretary of State, to magistrates in April, enjoining them to make full use of the military in the event of a riot. Thus the "massacre" was made to appear as an affair deliberately staged by a brutal and tyrannical Executive. All this helped to keep the agitation going, as instanced by the following news item of 4 July.

> At the sessions of the peace at Guildhall, a woman was tried for assaulting Mr. Emmerton, a constable, at St. Bride's parish. He had taken her into custody for bawling *Wilkes and Liberty*; when, for his folly, she said, she would take the liberty to break his head, which she accordingly did. The jury found her guilty, and the Court fined her one shilling.

More windows were broken in the City on Wilkes's birthday (28 October): but the next serious disturbance was caused by the court party itself. George Cooke, Wilkes's fellow-Member for Middlesex, died; and, in December, a new election was held, in which Serjeant Glynn, Wilkes's counsel, was opposed by Sir William Beauchamp Proctor, the Court candidate. Proctor, it later appeared, had hired a gang of Irish chairmen to "protect" him at the hustings. Whatever his own intentions, the brawl that they provoked led to the clubbing to death of George Clarke, a young Wilkesite lawyer, and two of the chairmen were later sentenced to death at the Old Bailey for his murder. Glynn was duly elected and the usual round of illuminations followed in the Strand and the City to celebrate another Wilkesite victory.

On 3 Feb. 1769, Wilkes was expelled from Parliament;

62 GEORGE RUDÉ

that night, there was a riot in Drury Lane, in the course of which "a number of persons riotously assembled" and "pulled down" some old houses before being dispersed by the guards. There followed, in swift succession, Wilkes's readoption by the Middlesex electors on 14 February and his unopposed return on the 16th; his further disqualification by the Commons on the 17th; his second unopposed election, after the withdrawal of Charles Dingley, on 16 March; its annulment by Parliament on the 17th and his further readoption on the 20th.

Just a month earlier, Wilkes's city friends, meeting at the London Tavern, had formed the Society of Supporters of the Bill of Rights. It was an historic occasion; yet the immediate object was merely to settle "Mr Wilkes's affairs"; and, on 7 March, it was agreed "that £300 be sent to Mr Wilkes for his immediate use". But no doubt it was the fear that the Society might become the centre of the Wilkesite political movement that prompted court supporters in the City to choose this moment for staging a "loyal" address to the King. The first meeting of the "loyalists" on 1 March was taken over by Wilkes's followers: but they persisted and presented their address, though with sadly depleted forces, at St James's Palace on 22 March. It provided Wilkes enthusiasts in the City and Westminster with a new occasion for vociferous protest. The "loyal" merchants, wrote the *Annual Register*,

> were interrupted by a desperate mob, on passing through the city, who insulted, pelted and maltreated the principal conductors; so that several coaches were

WILKES AND LIBERTY

obliged to withdraw, some to return back, others to proceed by bye-ways, and those who arrived at St. James's were so daubed with dirt, and shattered, that both masters and drivers were in the utmost peril of their lives.

In the Strand, [went on the report] a hearse with two white and two black horses took the lead of the cavalcade. On one side of the hearse were strikingly represented the soldiers firing at young Allen, and on the other the murder at Brentford. An attempt was made to drive it into the courtyard at St. James's; but the riot-act being read, it drove off to Carleton-house, afterwards to Cumberland-house, and last of all to Lord Weymouth's; at all of which places, the driver made a particular kind of compliment, and then retired.

Seventeen rioters were taken into custody: but all five of those indicted were discharged at the New Guildhall, Westminster, a week later.

This was the last great popular Wilkesite demonstration for many months. His return at Brentford for a fourth time on 13 April with nearly four times the vote of his opponent, Henry Lawes Luttrell, was, it is true, greeted by the march of "several thousand people" to the King's Bench prison, headed by "a number of horsemen, with colours flying and musick playing": but this was a very orderly affair; and even the Commons' decision, the next day, to disqualify Wilkes once more and to accept Luttrell as the elected Member for Middlesex provoked no popular outburst. Yet sympathy had not abated; and we are told that, when the King was at Epsom races in early May,

a fellow who stood near his Majesty had the audacity to hallow out, "Wilkes and Liberty for ever"!

64 GEORGE RUDÉ

The next months were taken up with political agitation of a different kind. The impetus given by the Society of Supporters of the Bill of Rights led to a campaign of petitions, remonstrances and addresses of "respectable" freeholders and burghers all over the country, while street-demonstrations of the "inferior set of people", whether in London or elsewhere, were in abeyance. In America, the cry of "Wilkes and Liberty" had, from the start, evoked a sympathetic response. While Wilkes was in gaol, the House of Assembly of South Carolina raised £1,500 towards the payment of his debts; in Boston, the Sons of Liberty sent him numerous messages of support, toasted him yearly at their Liberty Tree and, on his release from the King's Bench prison, drank the health of the "illustrious martyr of liberty" at a public banquet.

In England, too, Wilkes's release on 17 Apr. 1770, was greeted with "general & voluntary illuminations": but, reported the *Annual Register*, "to the praise of the lower order of patriots, no disorders have been complained of anywhere". It was only in the following March that the popular political movement started up again, this time over an issue in which Wilkes, while playing a prominent part, was no longer the central figure.

On 12 Mar. 1771, a proclamation read at the Royal Exchange called for the arrest of a number of printers and publishers who, in defiance of parliamentary privilege had printed and published certain proceedings of the House of Commons in half a dozen London journals. When the Commons messenger, armed with the Speaker's warrant, came to arrest John Miller, one of the printers,

WILKES AND LIBERTY

he was brought before the Lord Mayor, Brass Crosby, and Aldermen Wilkes and Richard Oliver, who not only discharged the printer but ordered the messenger to answer to a charge of assault. The Commons promptly commanded the three magistrates to appear before them —though having learned wisdom from experience, they did not press their invitation in the case of Wilkes. When the Lord Mayor and Alderman Oliver set out for Westminster on 19 March,

> a prodigious crowd of the better sort were at the Mansion-house and in the streets near it, who testified their approbation by repeated huzzas;

and, on their return that evening, the case having been deferred for a week, great crowds unharnessed their horses at St Paul's and drew their carriage in triumph to the Mansion House. The climax came on 27 March, when Lord Mayor Crosby (following Richard Oliver) was committed to the Tower for contempt of the House: that day, the King's State coach, passing down Parliament Street, was hailed with shouts of "No Lord Mayor, no King!" and the *Gentleman's Magazine* reported that

> Lord North lost his hat, and Mess. Fox's carriages were broken, their clothes torn, and greatly spattered with mud, by the incensed populace.[3]

The riots continued intermittently until the magistrates' release when Parliament was prorogued six weeks later.

Eighteen months were to pass before Wilkes himself

---

[3] Charles James Fox, who was, at this time, still a supporter of North, had incurred the particular displeasure of the "patriots" by urging the committal of Richard Oliver to the Tower.

became once more the centre of tumultuous demonstrations in the City. He had fallen out, since his release from prison, with his former allies, Alderman James Townsend and Richard Oliver; and the Rev John Horne. Oliver, while in the Tower, half refused to run in harness with him for the office of Sheriff. Wilkes had got his own back by topping the poll with 2,315 votes, while Oliver scored a mere 245; the same night, the effigy of Horne,

> in a canonical habit, with a pen in one hand and in the other a salt-box . . . was consumed in a bonfire, which the populace made for that purpose before the Mansion-house.

But far more violent disturbances attended the election of the Lord Mayor in October-November 1772. Wilkes, standing for the first time, was leading Townsend by 23 votes when the "popular "poll of the London Livery was declared on 6 October; but the final selection had, according to long-established custom, to be made from the two leading candidates by the Court of Aldermen. When, three weeks later, the Court declared in favour of Townsend, "the scene of confusion that ensued (was) inconceivable" but it was as nothing compared with the popular outburst that broke out on Lord Mayor's Day (9 November). That evening, when the new Lord Mayor returned to the Guildhall after his inaugural procession, a crowd of 3,000 filled the yard. Ladies arriving for the Lord Mayor's party were asked for money "to drink Mr Wilkes's health" and there were angry shouts of "It is Wilkes's turn" and "D—n my lord mayor, for a scoundrel, he has got Wilkes's right, and we will have

WILKES AND LIBERTY
67

him out". Distinguished visitors were molested by the rioters: "One gentleman I saw", stated a witness, "had part of his head of hair cut off." Bonfires were lit and the riots continued until two in the morning. The Hon. Artillery Company, whom the crowd (having first mistaken them for the Guards) treated with scant respect, took seven prisoners; of these, three appeared for trial at the Old Bailey, where two were acquitted and a third sentenced to five weeks in prison.

Two years later, in October 1774, Wilkes had his turn, and at his third attempt was elected Lord Mayor. "On this occasion", we are told,

> the joy of the populace was so great, that they took the horses from the coach, and, in the struggle for the honour of drawing it to the Mansion-house, one man lost his life and another was much hurt.

The unpopular Alderman Harley had his windows broken; and, on the morrow, Wilkes had the duty of committing the culprit for trial at the Old Bailey.

It was the last of the Wilkesite riots. Wilkes proved a highly successful and popular Lord Mayor. For some years, he retained the affection of the City craftsmen and journeymen: but his re-admission to Parliament in December 1774 opened up a new stage in his career, in which, while championing the cause of the American colonists and Parliamentary reform, he came to depend ever less on the support of the "inferior set of people". The link was finally broken when, in June 1780, he shouldered a musket and shot down rioters—composed, in the main, of the same social elements who, a dozen

years earlier, had shouted for "Wilkes and Liberty"—
at the height of the Gordon Riots. After 1783, he joined
Pitt and abandoned reform. A few years later, he greeted
the outbreak of the French Revolution with suitable
expressions of horror; he became reconciled to his old
enemy George III; and when he died in 1797, he had long
lived in the odour and sanctity of Toryism.

The "Wilkes and Liberty" movement had played its
part in the achievement of notable political successes: the
end of "general warrants", the right of electors to elect
the candidate of their choice and of editors to publish Parliamentary proceedings—not to mention the re-admission
of its author to Parliament and his election to numerous
City offices. In America, too, it had, no doubt, played
some part in stirring and shaping the combative spirit of
the colonists in their struggle for a redress of grievances
and for national independence. Further, for all its immaturity, it marks an important stage in the political
education of the "middling" and common people of
Britain and in the creation of a popular Radical tradition.
The political lessons learned in the 1760s and 1770s
seemed to have been largely forgotten in the confusion of
"No Popery" and the Gordon Riots; yet they were re-
vived, and bore richer fruit, in the 1790s under the
impact of the French Revolution, the factory system and
the work and writings of the democrats.

Ian R. Christie

CHARLES JAMES FOX [1]

Charles James Fox entered the House of Commons in 1768, while still under age. He made his mark at once as a debater; by his early thirties he was one of the leading personalities in the House, and he remained a member of it for over thirty-seven years, till his death in 1806. Yet his ministerial career is counted in months only, rather than in years: setting aside his early apprenticeship in junior posts, he held high Cabinet office for three months in 1782, eight months in 1783, and seven months in 1806—a year and a half in all. It seems at first sight extraordinary that a man of so much vitality, who commanded so much admiration from almost all who knew him, even from his opponents, possessed of dazzling Parliamentary talents, and with other abilities of no mean order, should have failed to achieve positions of place and power and, through them, to leave a greater mark upon his country's history.

Between 1774 and 1782, Fox spent eight years in opposition to the North ministry, and to its attempts to recover the American colonies. But, as a close analysis

[1] [Copyright © Ian R. Christie. Originally published in *History Today*, VIII (1958), pp. 110-18.]

of Parliamentary events makes clear, it was military defeat, and not his eloquence, that eventually brought down the Government. It is doubtful if the Economical Reform carried into law during 1782 owed much to his efforts; in any case, it was a grossly over-rated policy. As Secretary of State in 1783, he was responsible for concluding the Peace of Versailles, which ended the American War of Independence: but, having turned out Shelburne, who had laid the foundations of the treaty, he concluded it on rather less favourable terms than Shelburne had secured, and this in part through his own negligence. The East India Bill of 1783 was Burke's creation rather than Fox's: and both of them showed a remarkable political blindness in connexion with it, by laying themselves open to attack for seeking to engross political patronage. After being turned out of office in consequence, Fox in his opposition to the younger Pitt was, for the most part, frankly factious. He remained in opposition for all but the last few months of his life. During this part of his career, two measures are particularly associated with his name, the Libel Act and the abolition of the Slave Trade. He deserves praise for taking the lead over both these issues: but it must be remembered that, on the first, he had the active assistance of Pitt, and, on the second, Pitt's posthumous support, exerted through many of his friends and associates. The student of Fox is driven to the question, not, What did Fox accomplish? but, why was it that he accomplished so little?

Energy and ability Fox had in full measure; about this there can be no doubt. Even his most hostile critics never denied it. His brain seemed to work at twice the ordinary

CHARLES JAMES FOX

speed. "I believe," wrote his friend, Lord Carlisle, about 1771, "there never was a person yet created who had the faculty of reasoning like him. His judgments are never wrong; his decision is formed quicker than any man's I ever conversed with; and he never seems to mistake but in his own affairs." The French traveller, La Rochefoucauld, during his sojourn in England, noted that Fox amazed his contemporaries by the ease with which he mastered the intricacies of race-course betting. "To acquire all this knowledge," he wrote, "is so difficult, that those Englishmen who have mastered the various points regard it as quite extraordinary that Mr Fox should have been able, in five weeks of intensive study, to grasp its intricacies. In fact, they consider it to be evidence of the mastery of his genius." Philip Francis, a hostile observer, wrote that Fox was born for litigation and would have made his mark at the bar. His gift for absorbing facts and arguments was phenomenal, as was his ingenuity in debate. Of these powers he gave early proof. Horace Walpole relates, for instance, the proceedings in 1772, on Fox's motion for a Bill to amend the law regarding marriage, against which Lord North and Edmund Burke had both spoken with force and feeling:

> Charles Fox, who had been running about the House talking to different persons and scarce listening to Burke, rose with amazing spirit and memory, answered both Lord North and Burke, ridiculed the arguments of the former and confuted those of the latter with a shrewdness that, from its multiplicity of reasons, as much exceeded his father in embracing all the arguments of his antagonists, as he did in his manner and delivery.

Fox's gift in working up a brief is evident from many of the set-pieces with which he introduced a debate, notably his handling of his East India Bill. His capacity for debate is evident everywhere in the reports of his speeches. Carlisle and Francis, writing after his death, confirm what Walpole noted of his early career, the aggressive assurance with which he would attack the whole body of argument put up by his opponents. Francis remarked, that "of the judicial faculty as applied to penetration and destruction in argument", he had infinitely more than a common share. Fox was not a graceful orator, nor was his matter carefully arranged. He spoke with great rapidity, the words tumbling over each other in the hurry of self-expression, and with a good deal of repetition: but his vehemence, and the facility of argument that he employed, made a powerful impression, at least until the listener had time to consider carefully what he had said. The spontaneity, that ranged from sincere emotional appeal to the broadest clowning, enabled him always to hold the attention of the House of Commons.

Another quality, also, might have been thought to guarantee his success. No man was a better mixer; no man ever put on less side; no man had a greater talent for making strangers feel at their ease and for winning friendships. With justice did the younger Pitt refer to "the wand of the magician". Charm, affability, zest, overflowing spirits—these were qualities that disarmed all comers and captivated his friends: their strength is perhaps best seen in the reluctance with which men who had associated with him in politics for a decade or more,

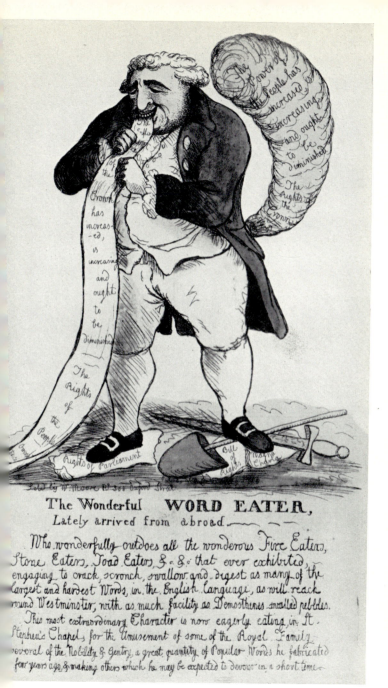

8. 1788. Fox adapting his principles as the illness of George III offers the prospect of office: he championed the Prince's hereditary right to become Regent.

9. 1796. Pitt and Dundas, unimpressed by John Bull's objections to the extra duty on wine recently announced in Pitt's budget.

CHARLES JAMES FOX

and who had for him the highest admiration and affection, gradually broke away when unable any longer to accept his lead on the issues raised by the French Revolution. Rarely has it been given to a man of such force of personality to stir up so few real hatreds in the course of his life.

Was he, then, unfortunate? Or was it some flaw in himself that barred him from success?

In 1783 George III admitted to William Grenville, that Fox was "a man of parts, quickness and great eloquence", but observed that he "wanted application, and consequently the fundamental knowledge necessary for business". One cannot simply take the King's word against Fox: their mutual dislike was notorious. But, in fact, there is a good deal of evidence to support this judgment. At times Fox displayed an enormous capacity for hard work: but he never showed himself capable of sustained effort on this scale. The will-power, the staying-power, the steady, grinding application, which make for greatness, were absent. Fox relied too much upon slap-dash improvisation; his bouts of energy were too liable to be extinguished by laziness and self indulgence. "Slap-dash improvisation" is not too harsh a phrase to describe his approach to public business. Well known is the early instance, in 1772, when he moved for, and obtained leave to introduce, a Bill for the repeal of Lord Hardwicke's Marriage Act, without having taken the first step to prepare any Bill on the subject: and, at a later stage, he arrived from Newmarket so late on the day that the second reading was to be taken that the Bill was thrown out in his absence.

P.P.—F

His attendance at public boards tells the same story. Ambitious young politicians would have given much to be appointed, as Fox was, to the Board of Admiralty, when barely twenty-one. Most of them would have made more of their chance. But, for the first three months, Fox was rarely there; for the next four or five he attended regularly, evidently alternating with other members under vacation arrangements; and then, for the remaining nineteen months of his appointment, there was almost complete withdrawal—during twelve of these months he made no attendance at all. Over the same period, although he intervened frequently in debate on any subject that caught his interest, there is scarcely a trace of evidence that he made any attempt to take his share as a spokesman for the Admiralty in the House of Commons. A little later, the chart of his attendance after appointment to the Treasury Board seems to have begun following much the same course, though his tenure was too short for this evidence to be considered conclusive.

True, when Fox left the Treasury, he was only twenty-five. All this might be regarded youthful peccadillo. But there are later examples of impetuosity, carelessness, inattention to detail. There was the case in 1778, when he decided to undertake an attack upon the Government over the fiasco of Saratoga. "I have business enough," he wrote to his friend, Fitzpatrick, "indeed, more than I can well manage; for though I like the House of Commons itself, I hate the preparatory business of looking at accounts, drawing motions, etc., as much as you could do." In his haste, he launched his attack on the ministers prematurely, before the military leaders concerned had

CHARLES JAMES FOX

returned from America and could be called on to give information. Small wonder that his efforts misfired for lack of evidence. After his resignation in 1782, at the end of his three months' tenure of the Foreign Office, his successor, Grantham, remarked, "he certainly was precipitate in many measures". This might be discounted as mere prejudice: but then, in 1783, there was the glaring omission in the preparation of diplomatic instructions that gave away a substantial point in negotiation to the court of Spain. "We made a concession not warranted by the preliminaries", Fox wrote to the British ambassador at Paris, and candidly owned his fault: "the unfortunate circumstance, too, of my having left this article quite blank in my project, prevented the words coming into consideration in the same manner as those of the other articles"[2]. "Inexcusable" would be perhaps a juster epithet. No statesman or politician is immune from mistakes, and Fox must have his allowance. But there is a consistency of evidence that seems to support the King's condemnation of him as lacking in the application necessary for public business.

An equally grave fault was his reckless lack of judgment. This was early apparent. As a schoolboy, listening to a debate in the House of Lords, he was noted by Lord Mansfield in an aside to his neighbour: "Fox's son, Charles, with twice his parts and half his sagacity." His impetuosity seemed to increase through the years rather than being subdued with maturity. In the opinion of George III, in 1783, he was "totally destitute of discretion

[2] Manchester to Fox, 15 July, Fox to Manchester, 20 July 1783, Brit. Mus. Add. MSS. 47562, ff. 90, 96.

and sound judgment". Once more, there is plenty of evidence throughout Fox's career to justify the King's view. Time and again, he seemed incapable of pausing and taking a balanced view of circumstances, and would insist upon going his own way with disastrous results. At the very outset of public life, he threw away a fair prospect of ministerial advancement, not on any question of principle, but from ungovernable pique against Lord North. During 1773 he became involved in one of the undertakings of Edmund Burke's disreputable brother, Richard—a land speculation in the Caribbean island of St Vincent. He was engaged to press Richard's claims with the Treasury, and, as an inducement and reward, was offered a share in the profits in the event of success. Circumstances were such that North could do nothing for him; and, from about the end of the year, Fox, bitter with disappointment, seems to have regarded himself as cheated and treacherously deceived by him. In January 1774 he gave up all attendance at the Treasury Board, and in the following weeks his behaviour in the Commons is consistent with only one explanation—that, in retaliation, he intended to embarrass North as far as lay in his power; and it was for this reason that he lost his seat on the Treasury Board.

This circumstance explains also the vituperative personal hostility towards North that is apparent in Fox's speeches during the following years. He certainly did not break with North over American affairs. At that moment, North was bringing forward his proposals for punitive legislation against the people of Massachusetts, consequent upon the news of the Boston Tea Party and

CHARLES JAMES FOX

other incidents. Fox, for at least a fortnight after his dismissal, was still speaking in support of the proposal to close the port of Boston, though he was trying to make trouble for North over its details—notably the grant of a delegated power to the Crown, to re-open the port when amends had been made. It was only after some weeks that he finally went into open opposition to government policy in America. Evidence from reports of debates[3] confirms the later account by Lord Carlisle: "If an idle quarrel had not happened between him and Lord North, we might have seen him a supporter of the American War, a champion for the prerogatives of the Crown, and a favourite in the Closet . . . the consequence was the converting a most powerful and attached friend into a bitter enemy, a driving him into the arms of a faction, the principles of which he adopted not from inclination but from resentment. Five days before that event, he was held by the opposition in execration, and in return those who composed that faction in contempt by him."[4] These were the circumstances, and not the malice or the fear suspected by Fox's biographer, Sir George Otto Trevelyan, that led George III to condemn Fox, with the observation: "Indeed that young man has so thoroughly cast off every principle of common honour and honesty that he must become as contemptible as he is odious."

---

[3] Speeches of 14 and 25 Mar. 1774, on the Boston Port Bill, Brickdale MSS., Diary, x, 22: Debrett, *Parliamentary Debates*, 1743-4, vii, 92-3.

[4] Character of Fox, by Lord Carlisle (1806), Carlisle MSS. My thanks are due to Professor A. Aspinall, for permitting me to quote this passage from his transcripts of the Carlisle MSS.

Fox thus turned to opposition to the North ministry during the American War of Independence. His attacks upon it in the Commons dwelt mainly upon the impossibility of reconquering America, and upon the incompetence of ministers in the waging of war. None of this necessarily damned his political future: the younger Pitt came into Parliament in 1780, pursuing much the same conduct, and in little over three years he was Prime Minister. But Fox could not restrain his impulses and his passions. He developed a personal hostility towards George III, which could only be assuaged by the King's complete surrender to him in political matters. This, in every way, was a mistake. It led Fox to vent his spleen in private conversation in a manner that was bound to get to the King's ear and cause exasperation; in the spring and summer of 1782, in speech and writing, he and his circle were referring to the King as "Satan"; and on one occasion, after the fall of the North ministry, he was reported as saying: "Certainly things look well, but he (meaning the King) will die soon, and that will be best of all." It led him to attribute far too much importance to the part played by the King in prolonging the American War, and to think that it was the King alone who stood in the way of a ministry that would get rid of the war by conceding independence to America. There was a Parliamentary majority in favour of the war: but Fox got over this difficulty by maintaining that it was a corrupt and hired majority, created by "the influence of the Crown". Nothing could have been farther from the truth. As Burke and other opposition leaders from time to time admitted, the country was behind Parliament in

CHARLES JAMES FOX 79

its approval of the continued efforts to reconquer the colonies. In all this Fox sadly deceived himself about the forces that sustained a war ministry in office until after the military catastrophe of Yorktown.

Between 1780 and 1784, in the years of political crisis provoked by the loss of America, Fox's opportunism was seen at its worst. For the advantage of the moment, he snatched at constitutional conceptions that were mutually exclusive. On the one hand, he plunged headlong into the radical movement in the City of Westminster, in association with men who wished to make the House of Commons much more subordinate to opinion outside, by means of electoral reform and more frequent general elections. In April 1780, he delivered himself of the view that, "when the representative body did not speak the sense of the constituent, the voice of the latter was constitutional and conclusive"; and he even pledged himself to work for annual Parliaments. On the other hand, later on, in 1784, when it better suited his purpose, he upheld against outside opinion the right of a given Parliamentary majority (one which he led) to have its own way and to coerce the King into restoring the coalition ministry to office.

This majority, by means of which he sought to dictate during the opening months of 1784, was that created by his junction with North in the notorious coalition Government of 1783. That coalition is yet another instance of his lack of judgment. It shattered the confidence of many independent members of the Commons, who had thought that in Fox they had discovered a man of principle, and who were aghast at his joining

80 IAN R. CHRISTIE

forces with politicians whom he had previously denounced in the most forthright terms, declaring that he could never associate in office with them. Fox's words, it was clear, could not be taken on trust. Indeed, he said many things that he did not mean, and, to make points in debate, appealed to principles of action on which he held no real convictions. There are other instances. In 1779, he lashed out in debate at Lord Amherst, the commander-in-chief, on the ground that he was ruining the army by permitting political influence to govern military promotions: but in 1783, as Secretary of State, he clashed seriously with Conway, because Conway, as commander-in-chief, resisted his and Portland's attempts to make political promotions.[5] Again, in the years 1780 to 1782, no one was more vehement than Fox in denunciation of the use of patronage for political purposes. And yet, were Fox and his colleagues so entirely innocent of intention to engross patronage through his East India Bill? When William Eden, one of the leading spirits in the formation of the coalition, set out to persuade John Courtenay of the merits of the measure, he "expatiated with great zeal and party confidence on the infinite advantages of this politic expedient for infallibly securing the permanency of the present Administration for seven years at least, by their possessing such an unbounded and lucrative patronage".[6]

But perhaps Fox's greatest errors in these years were to think that the King should be excluded altogether from

[5] Conway to Fox, 31 Jul., 7 Aug. 1783, Add. MSS. 47568, ff. 144-51.
[6] John Courtenay, *Incidental Anecdotes and a Biographical Sketch* (London 1809), 135-8.

CHARLES JAMES FOX

politics—that is, that he should no longer have a voice in the selection of ministers—and to believe, that the events of 1782 had made this possible: in March 1782 he even boasted, that he had brought about "a complete change in the constitution". This was to traverse cherished conceptions about the balance of forces in the constitution which any but party men were bound to defend. In 1784, one of the most damaging counts against him with the public was that he had denied the King his legitimate role in the system of government. Fox's actions in these years reflect an inadequate grasp of political and constitutional realities and an insensitiveness to public opinion. This, added to the personal hostility which the King, not unreasonably, had developed towards him, led to his complete undoing in 1784.

In the years immediately following 1784 Fox carried on an opposition to Pitt that was more factious than enlightened. In 1785 he and his friends conducted an unscrupulous campaign to prevent Pitt from succeeding with his proposals for a commercial agreement with Ireland, stirring up nationalist passions on both sides of the Irish Sea; and in 1786, he unsuccessfully opposed the liberal commercial treaty negotiated with France. But within five years he had again exposed himself to damaging attack—to being "unwhigged"—by championing the Prince of Wales's claim to assume the Regency during the mental illness of George III. Later, in 1792 and 1793, his resentment against Pitt and George III was such that he would not contemplate the chance of taking second place in a coalition, and persisted in an opposition which became more and more unreasonable.

At the end of 1792, such was his state of mind that he "declared with an oath, that there was no address at this moment Pitt could frame, he would not propose an amendment to, and divide the House upon". His belief that the security precautions taken by Pitt's Government, against the spread of revolutionary ideas from France, betokened the extinction of liberty in Britain may have been sincere: but it was certainly based on self-delusion; and his public pronouncements in debate on the subject of France during the Revolutionary Wars attributed to French leaders an innocence of intention to damage British interests which has been imperceptible to most other observers and writers then and since. It is not surprising that he remained in the political wilderness, the leader of a tiny and ineffectual opposition, for practically the remainder of his life.

If any further explanation is to be sought for his failure, it is probable that it is to be found in an indiscipline fundamental to his nature, and given full play owing to the defects of his upbringing, which marred all his gifts and generous impulses. The blame lies with his father, Henry Fox, who utterly spoiled and also corrupted his favourite son. Nothing that the infant Charles would do was denied him, whether it were making a blaze on the fire with state papers, or smashing a watch regardless of its cost. Nothing was done at home that might in any way inculcate in him discipline and an understanding of its advantages, or a sense of the external realities with which every human being must come to terms. Instead, the view of his father was, "Let nothing be done to break his spirit. The world will do that business fast enough."

CHARLES JAMES FOX

Nothing could have been more disastrous than such indulgence, especially when accompanied by an early introduction to the vices of fashionable society. When barely fourteen, Charles was taken for four months away from Eton, to accompany his father on a tour of the Continent. He returned so confirmed a gambler that the tone of the school suffered a long-enduring change for the worse as a result of his influence. Ever after he had the gambler's indifference to people and circumstances. This is the key to an understanding of him; and we are fully justified in dwelling upon it. There was the disregard for his father: no one ever showed less filial duty, in the way he squandered his father's fortune. There was the disregard for his friends, from whom he borrowed shamelessly, overwhelming them with storms of emotional reproaches when they showed reluctance to help him: it was pointed out to one of them, Carlisle, in 1774, that it was time Fox showed some consideration for his affairs—"Your future friendship will then have a basis (on) which it has never yet stood, and that is reciprocity." When the crash came, his debts amounted to £140,000. After this there was talk of his training and earning a living at the bar; and, had he had the strength of character to do it, there is no doubt he would have made a brilliant and successful barrister. But it all ended in smoke; and having let others ruin him, the most constructive effort to which he eventually could rise, in the years 1781-2, was to recoup his fortunes by the ruin of others, running with three cronies a faro bank which in good times might bring in as much as £2,000 a week.

The gambler's nature was dominated by disregard for

people and for facts: it was in this sense that Fox, although he gave up the card tables after 1784, remained a gambler for the rest of his life. For disregard of facts, there is his remarkable avowal in a letter to Burgoyne in 1778: "At whist, as you very well know, it is often right in a desperate case to play upon a supposition of your partner's having a good hand, though there might be the strongest symptoms of the contrary; because if he has not the game is lost. Just so, I think of the present state of affairs. It is the duty of those who mean to act upon public motives to suppose many things which they cannot believe." For his disregard of people, there is the testimony of two of the men who knew him well. When he was in his thirties, George Selwyn, one of his more critical admirers, wrote of him:

> Charles, I am persuaded, would have no consideration on earth but for what was useful to his own ends. You have heard me say, that I thought he had no malice or rancour; I think so still and am sure of it. But I think that he has no feeling, neither, for anyone but himself; and if I could trace in any one action of his life anything that had not for its object his own gratification, I should with pleasure receive the intelligence, because then I had much rather (if it were possible) think well of him than not.

Beside this we may set the observation of Philip Francis: "The essential defect in his character, and the cause of all his failures, strange as it may seem, was that he had no heart."

The politician moves, and has his being, in a close-meshed web of human ideals and aspirations, ideas and

CHARLES JAMES FOX

prejudices. He must respond to the vibrations of numerous threads, each running back to some individual source. For such comprehensive and delicate perception Fox's mind was not attuned. He was constitutionally ill-adapted to come to terms with people and circumstances. Consequently, his political judgment was blind and disastrous for himself and his followers. Not all his febrile energy, fertile intelligence, mental ingenuity, and dexterity with words, could compensate for this defect. As a politician he was his own worst enemy.

Esmond Wright

HENRY DUNDAS
"Harry the Ninth" [1]

Boswell was not alone in his tribute to Dundas, if tribute it was. "The whole country was managed by the indisputed and sagacious energy of a single native, who knew the circumstances, and the wants, and the proper bait, of every countryman worth being attended to," wrote Cockburn. "Henry Dundas, the first Viscount Melville, was the Pharos of Scotland. Who steered upon him was safe; who disregarded the light was wrecked."[2] Yet the phenomenal career of Harry the Ninth has been little appreciated by historians. Born three years before the '45 and before the curbing of the Highlands, and eighteen years before Scotchmen were butts for political ridicule in London, he was yet, before he was fifty, to run the affairs of Scotland and India, and simultaneously to direct the War with Revolutionary and Napoleonic France, and the war against the forces of revolution at

[1] [Copyright © Esmond Wright. Originally published in *History Today*, VIII (1958) pp. 155-63.]

[2] Lord Cockburn, *Life of Lord Jeffrey*, Vol. I, p. 77 (Edinburgh 1852).

HENRY DUNDAS

home. Not the least striking feature in Henry Dundas's career is that he built it avowedly on being a Scot and an "English Scot", who yet refused to cultivate an English accent. And long before Professor Namier taught us to study "interest", Dundas's strength lay—even after his impeachment—in his "connexion" and in his influence. He is a case-study in eighteenth-century political method; and he gives a foretaste of those administrative talents that Lowland Scots were to bring to British and Imperial affairs in the next one hundred and fifty years.

Not that the talents were ever fully appreciated. For Dundas always had enemies, rivals, and critics. And, along with the charges of peculation to which the impeachment gave a certain justice, the core of the criticism was essentially that he lacked principles in politics, that he was a manager of men, a more competent—and less fawning —Newcastle, a Scottish Walpole. This view has at times been carried to extravagant lengths, as by Sir John Fortescue.

> Buoyancy was of the essence of the man. Principle with him was a kind of water-ballast, to be pumped in or pumped out, according to the requirements of the moment in respect of trim, stability and freeboard . . . I am forced to write down Dundas as a born wire-puller. . . . No man could more shrewdly perceive the tendencies of the moment in political affairs, nor divine more cunningly whether it would be most profitable to oppose them, to follow them, or to lead them. Such power implies intimate sympathy with the commonplace mind, intimate knowledge of the commonplace nature, boundless command of commonplace ability, boundless wealth in commonplace resource. . . . Yet the

88 ESMOND WRIGHT

commonplace, though raised, as mathematicians say, to infinity, remains the commonplace and can never soar above it.[3]

And much more of this sort. Our own age, like Dundas's own, has a shrewder appreciation of the motive forces in politics, and can find fascination in "commonplace" stories like his.

The roots of Dundas's strength always lay in Scotland, as Hume Brown pointed out in his History[4]: in the prestige of his family, in his own personal qualities, and in the political condition of the country. His father, grandfather, and great-grandfather before him had all served on the Scottish bench; at the time of his birth, his father was Lord President of the Court of Session, and when he was himself called to the Scottish Bar in 1763, a half-brother had succeeded his father as President in turn. Scots lawyers had long honoured the Dundases of Arniston in Midlothian. What a training in law failed to do the General Assembly could remedy. It gave Henry Dundas a platform on which to develop those talents for public-speaking of which many an English Ministry was to stand in need. "'Twas in Kirk-Courts he learn'd his airs" became part of the criticism of him later.[5] He was

[3] Sir John Fortescue, *British Statesman of the Great War, 1793-1814* (Oxford, 1911), pp. 51, 59. Cf. the same author's *History of the British Army*, Vol. IV, Part I (London 1915), pp. 71-2 *et seq.*

[4] *History of Scotland*, III, 347.

[5] Cf. G. W. T. Omond's reference: "What Marathon was to Athens, what the Metaurus was to Rome, what Morgarten is to Switzerland, that the long fight of the Church against the Crown is to Scotland . . . the General Assembly had an importance in Scotland which no gathering of churchmen could ever have in England." *The Lord Advocates of Scotland*, Vol. II (Edinburgh 1883), p. 84.

DISSOLUTION; or — The Alchymist producing an Aetherial Representation

10. 1796. Pitt prepares for a general election: Crown influence and Treasury money are to produce a subservient House, with himself as dictator and his own crest in place of the royal arms.

The GIANT-FACTOTUM amusing himself.

11. 1797. Pitt in the House of Commons, playing with the world: his right foot is supported by Wilberforce and Dundas, his left crushes Fox and the opposition.

HENRY DUNDAS

indeed slow to commit himself completely to politics; the law had great appeal—and offered almost as rewarding a prospect. He was appointed Solicitor-General in 1766 and Dean of the Faculty of Advocates in Edinburgh in 1776. He was hesitant to surrender the office of Dean of the Faculty even after his career in London was well launched—he saw it as "a badge of his connexion" amid "the vicissitudes of politicks". He held on to it until 1785. The connexion, like the caution, was native to him.

In the general election of 1774, however, Dundas was elected for the county of Midlothian, and he continued a member of Parliament without intermission until his elevation to the peerage as Viscount Melville in 1802; until 1790 he represented the county and afterwards the city of Edinburgh. Although he was often on holiday in Midlothian, and after 1783 on his new estate at Dunira in the Earn valley in Perthshire, from 1774 onwards his base of operations was London. In 1787 he bought a villa on Wimbledon Common, among the political gentry—a villa with a room reserved for the use of Mr Pitt. If the roots—like the accent—remained in the Lothians, the point at which the pressure was exercised was in Westminster and Downing Street. As Dr Johnson was constrained to admit, Dundas's accent was "of no small use to him, as it rouses the attention of the House by its uncommonness; and is equal to tropes and figures in a good English speaker".

From the first, Dundas recognised this two-edged strength; and though the attacks on his Scottishness continued, his career marks the effective merger of

P.P.—G

English and Scottish politics. Physically tougher and more skilled in debate than Bute, he was as patient and phlegmatic in controversy as North, and craggily handsome; Parliamentary attacks broke against him as water against Scottish stone. The Scots around Bute, like Wedderburn and Elliot, had been lightweights by comparison. And Dundas identified his politics more closely with London than did Bute; the load of administration he bore in the years from 1784 onwards made the old taunts increasingly inapt; his speeches were weighty and well-informed, though rarely eloquent; his knowledge of the War Office, of Indian affairs and—by 1800—of the map of the world, formidable. Until his time Scottish members spoke little, and normally only on topics concerning Scotland. Dundas took a wider view. Behind the friendship with Pitt the Younger there was a deeper respect for the Britain Pitt the Elder had created; after 1763 new prospects for Scots were opening up in the Empire that Pitt had won. Glasgow and the tobacco lords, Edinburgh, the lawyers and the gentry prospered. In politics Dundas was the first to take advantage of these opportunities, the first to accept the Act of Union and to make it the centre of his system.

Like his Scots predecessors, however—and like most of his contemporaries—he was an "independent" in politics. He described himself in 1781, after six years in office with North, as "an unprejudiced, unconnected man". Much of the criticism visited upon him by Whig historians has been due to their failure to appreciate Dundas's highly Namierist view of politics. He was, especially under North, building a reputation, a Scotsman

HENRY DUNDAS 91

on the make. His first letter to North in 1771 explained that he was likely to be elected: but it neither promised partisan support nor solicited favours. Members of Parliament with talents to offer—by no means the whole House in any century—were as valuable to a Ministry as it, in turn, might be to them; the political assumptions of the time were atomic and individualist; members might group themselves around particular nuclei, but in restlessly changing form. Political advancement through disposal of one's talents was taken for granted in a House of Commons not yet built on partisan principles, and in which administrations were normally "wide", to use the eighteenth-century term, rather than "narrow". Administration was formed, as North and Thurlow both told Dundas, "out of inveterate factions jealous of each other, and united only by the desire of getting into office". Hence the coalitions, "the unions of abilities", "the Ministries of all the Talents", the "broad-bottomed Administrations". Nor had "issues" as yet come permanently to divide men, nor yet to be strongly social or economic. If Dundas was frequently criticised as inconsistent, so were all his Scots predecessors—and so were North and Fox and Pitt in turn.

In North's Ministry, Dundas displayed his debating talents. For the most part he loyally supported the American War, and spoke frankly—and probably truly—when he said in 1777, in reply to Fox, that "to bring America to reason we must make her feel our power". He was too late: next day came the news of Saratoga. But he continued an advocate of force, even of temporary dictatorship—to North's and the King's embarrassment in 1778. He always favoured "strength" and "activity" in Governments. Important though advancement might be, independence had its advantages too. And the talents were valued by—indeed, essential to—Ministries. In 1779 he was appointed Keeper of the Signet of Scotland, which in 1782 became a sinecure for life—expressly, as the King said, "that Lord North might be certain of an able debater at all times in the House of Commons". Wraxall thought him North's "most powerful auxiliary". Wilberforce described him not only as "the first speaker on the ministerial side", but referred particularly to "a manliness in his character which prevents his running away from the question". Dundas never forgot this first —and hardest—rule of debate: to fight opponents on their own ground. "Manly" was frequently applied to him, even if his was a manliness, as Wraxall said, sometimes "tinged with convivial purple". He had need of this quality in 1781, when he confessed that it was now impossible to defeat America. His "independence", not for the first time, earned him black looks from the King. It won him a reputation, however: and that, long before the appearance in the House, in 1781, of Pitt the Younger.

But Dundas's skill on the floor was only one half of his strength. The other lay north of the Tweed. He was not only a debater but, since 1775, Lord Advocate. He held this office as Ministries changed, with Rockingham, with Shelburne and even for a short time with the Fox-North Coalition. Under Shelburne he was also Treasurer of the Navy, and in control of all the patronage of Scotland. When the Coalition was dismissed by the King in December 1783, it was Dundas and Pitt who bore the

HENRY DUNDAS

brunt of the Opposition attacks for three months. In sixteen divisions, each angrier than the last, Pitt's Government was defeated. He steadily refused either to resign office or to dissolve Parliament. When the majority against him was reduced to a single vote, the Government went to the country, to Pitt's great, if carefully managed, triumph. Dundas's reward had already been given him, the office of Treasurer of the Navy. This contest not only saw the beginning of the long alliance between the two men, but it brought out the importance to all Ministries, including Pitt's, of the Dundas connexion. This continued until Dundas's death, and was due essentially to the pre-representative character of eighteenth-century politics, especially north of the Border.

Dundas's brother had been approached by the Duke of Newcastle in 1765, on the formation of Rockingham's first Ministry, to manage Scotland on his behalf. He had refused, being a judge: but the approach indicated the influence of the family, and the nature of politics. The Dundases lived near Edinburgh; they were all lawyers and gentry; their neighbours were the Buccleuchs, the Hopetouns, the Elliots. These groups of related men managed the franchise. There were forty-five members of Parliament, thirty elected for the Scottish counties, fifteen for the towns. The burgh members were chosen by the town-councillors. In the counties, only those could vote who were listed on the roll of freeholders as holding land directly from the Crown. The practice had grown by which the larger landowners transferred their superiority nominally to other persons—and thus

94 ESMOND WRIGHT

dominated the elections. In any event, electors were few. The *Confidential Report of 1788*, drawn up to help William Adam and Henry Erskine to organise the Whigs against Dundas, gives "the political opinions, family connexions or personal circumstances" of all county voters in Scotland; and it establishes that there were in the thirty-three counties in 1788 only 2,662 voters. Of these approximately half were merely "parchment barons". Three counties were permanently disfranchised—Bute and Caithness by turns, Nairn and Cromarty by turns, Clackmannan and Kinross by turns. Every other county "elected" one member. Ayrshire was the most "democratic", having 205 electors, Fife had 187, Argyll 42, Bute 12. There were 93 voters on the roll for Midlothian in 1788; and this account of their leanings would serve as prototype for any Cook County precinct captain:

Thomas Brown of Nether Ploughlands.
 A middling estate. A family. Connected with John Gray, W.S. Will go with Mr. Dundas.

William Miller of Craigentinny.
 The Quaker. Rich and independant.

Sir Andrew Lauder Dick, of Grange, Baronet.
 A very good estate. Married Miss Brown of Johnstonburn. Much under the influence of George Cumin, W.S., his cousin.

John Russel of Roseburn, W.S.
 Rich. A Family. A brother of Claude Russel from India. Has a son who was made Agent for Teinds for Mr. Dundas.

Thomas Sivright of Southhouse.
 A pretty good estate. Could make two or three votes. Not married. A very recluse man.

HENRY DUNDAS

The *Report* lists twenty-seven "principal interests in this County", from the Duke of Buccleuch to Lord Torphichen, but concludes:

> It will take a very powerful Combination to shake the interest of Mr. Dundas of Melville, the Treasurer of the Navy, the present member for the County, who can make three votes on his own estate, and who, independant of the interest of his family (Dundas of Arniston), has great influence in this County, though there are also many who are not his friends.[6]

This, rather than "principle" or oratory, was the root of Dundas's strength in Edinburgh: in his first election he won 57 votes against 21 (including his own) for his opponent, Sir Alexander Gilmour. Thereafter he was rarely opposed. Electorates being small, influence was easy; other members being elected by the same system, in small closed groups, influence upon them from Edinburgh and London was also easy. By 1783 the Lord Advocate had become the channel through which appointments were made—and further influence exercised. This power grew steadily over the next twenty years. Professor Holden Furber has calculated that, in the Parliament of 1784, 22 of Scotland's 45 members were attached to the Dundas interest, in 1790 at least 32, and in 1797 as many as 36. In 1797 his power was at its highest, for 13 of the 16 representative peers were also his friends.[7] It was in 1797 that he made the claim that, if he exerted himself thoroughly, he might be able "to

---

[6] *The Political State of Scotland in 1788*, ed. by Sir Charles Elphinstone Adam of Blair-Adam, Bt. (Edinburgh 1887), p. 109.

[7] Holden Furber, *Henry Dundas, First Viscount Melville 1742-1811* (O.U.P., 1931), Appendix A.

prevent the return of any one member for Scotland hostile to Government". He was, in his own phrase, "a cement of political strength" from "a variety of circumstances". These included the unrepresentative system, the clan loyalties of politics, and the use of patronage. And, in some degree, these were—until 1832—hereditary: much of his influence, though little of his skill, was passed on to his son. But such a system was, nevertheless, personal; it depended not on the office but on the man. From the beginning, Dundas had emphasised that it was not the office of King's Advocate that gave him his power. "In my hands", he wrote in 1782, "it was a very good concomitant, but in itself independant of talent and consequence in the House of Commons I hold it as nothing". The Scottish bloc was powerful reinforcement to Government in Westminster; it was equally held together from Westminster rather than from Edinburgh, and was serving further to pull the two countries together, whatever its undemocratic character. It was in London that prestige was won. "Whatever little consequence and distinction I have, if I have any", he said in 1784, "I derive entirely from this House."

The "rankest of all Scotchmen", as Horace Walpole described him, thus brought great strength to Pitt's Ministry in 1784. And in it he grew into a gifted administrator. Since 1781 he had taken an interest in Indian affairs—more than once he came close to being appointed Governor-General. In the next decade the offices piled up—Treasurer of the Navy (1784-1800), Home Secretary (1791-4), Member, then President of the Board of Control (1784-1801), Secretary of War (1794-1801), and

HENRY DUNDAS

after his peerage, in Pitt's second administration, First Lord of the Admiralty (1804-5). His interests ranged from the *zemindar* system in Bengal to the Reform riots of Dundee and Edinburgh, and from patronage at home to tactics in the Mediterranean and the Caribbean. The affairs of the country were, from 1784 to 1806, essentially in the hands of a triumvirate, Pitt, Grenville, and Dundas, or of two connexions, the Grenvilles and the Dundases. If Pitt as captain commanded the ship and, in the end, weathered the storm, it was often Dundas, as commander, who ran it. His administrative talents outmatched Pitt's, not least after 1792, when reform was abandoned. He could work hard, without calling on the immense nervous energy that Pitt needed—in 1801 Dundas feared for Pitt's sanity, and he was dead, burned-out, at the age of forty-six, five years later. For the older man, the burden had been lightened in 1801, when he went out of office with Pitt; and in 1802 he went to the Lords as Viscount Melville.

About these years as a colleague of Pitt, the most critical years in British history except for 1940, various myths have grown. Three in particular need correction. The first is that Dundas owed his rise to the association with Pitt. As we have seen, this is belied by the success Dundas won in the Commons in the seven years before Pitt appeared there. It was on Dundas's advice that North threw in his hand in 1782. He had been involved in all the negotiations of the years 1781-3, and devised various re-groupings; if he was impressed by Pitt's talents, he was not alone in that. He sought to put Pitt in office in February and March 1783; he succeeded in

98 ESMOND WRIGHT

December. He was, in fact, indispensable to the formation of any stable government—and by 1781 he knew it.

The second charge that needs correction is that Dundas was uniformly illiberal, that here was the malign force that drove Pitt towards reaction. This view is far too simple. The points on which he had marched out of step with North until 1781, and in doing so permanently lost the affection of the King, were in essence the issues of reform, few though they were and minor matters though they appeared to Dundas. Yet, in his first year as a Lord Advocate, he had promoted a bill to break down the conditions of serfdom in which Scots colliers worked; he completed this measure in 1799. He sought "to cherish and make the proper use of the Highlands of Scotland"; in 1775 he began his nine-year campaign for the return of the old proprietors; he argued that the Highlanders were ideal military material and should be treated with sympathy. In 1779, under the influence of Adam Smith, he showed sympathy with the idea of free trade with Ireland.[8] He had, indeed, more sympathy with Ireland than had most English ministers—for he was essentially a Unionist. Although he opposed general and vague schemes of Parliamentary reform, he gave limited support to Pitt's proposals in 1785: the specific always appealed to Dundas. Not, however, when it came too close to home. With storm-clouds mounting over France, he opposed Sheridan's proposals in 1789 for the reform of the Scots burghs and poured scorn on ideas of popular sovereignty. He was ready to send convicts to Botany Bay, and was

---

[8] *Brit. Mus. Add. MSS.* Auckland Papers, No. 34416, ff. 470, 472, for Dundas-Adam Smith correspondence.

HENRY DUNDAS

vindictive in punishments. Without defending slavery or the slave trade, he thought that the abolition of either would be an act of self-denial by Britain that would lose her a commerce other nations would then acquire—and it would thus be of little value to the Negro. Nevertheless, he favoured the gradual abolition of the trade. If his motives in recalling Hastings from India—as a possible rival—were open to suspicion, he tried, like Pitt, to maintain a judicial point of view; and he said much in his favour at his trial. He showed a politician's knowledge of the Oriental mind at the impeachment: a bribe, he thought, was in the East merely "to be considered as a sort of ceremonial of intercourse". Originally sympathetic to toleration for Roman Catholics, he was frightened into quiescence by the riots of Edinburgh and the protests of Glasgow; yet, in 1793 and 1800, he showed himself sympathetic to religious—and political—reform in Ireland. In 1801 he was franker than Pitt himself on the need for Catholic emancipation. These to-and-fros are not the testament of a dedicated man; there were few crusaders in eighteenth-century politics, and Dundas would not have chosen to be of their company. He was first and last a realist, a defender of his own *status quo*, but ready now and then to give ground in a modest way. He was not pliant but, equally, he was not pliable: there was in him a solid core of Scots commonsense.

The third point on which the record needs clarifying is Dundas's contribution to war-time strategy. The policies of Pitt after 1793 have been almost universally condemned by historians, highly though the man has been himself esteemed: the scattering of forces, the "breaking of windows with guineas", the succession of military defeats. On the other hand, except for the mutinies of 1797, the Navy's was an impressive record, for which the Treasurer and later First Lord could take some credit. But what marked Dundas's period of war-service, from 1793 to 1801, was its Imperial emphasis. Here again the moving force was not the younger, but the elder, Pitt. On lines that recalled 1757-9, Dundas was ready to take advantage of every turn in the war to strike at France overseas: he fought the decision to abandon Minorca and the Mediterranean; he pressed the importance of the West Indies; he was responsible for the seizure of Mauritius and the Cape; he backed Miranda's schemes for the liberation of Spanish America; and, not least, he planned and carried out the Egyptian campaign of 1801 against the advice of both Pitt and the King. It is impossible but to feel that, on the wider front overseas, Dundas had a surer grasp and greater foresight than his younger master. The territories—and the trade—won in 1815, and the nineteenth-century Empire that followed from them, owed as much to his planning as to Pitt's leadership or to Nelson's and Wellington's courage.

The final years, despite the long-looked-for and much-protested-against peerage were years of anticlimax and of drama. The impeachment was, in part, a political gambit of the Whigs; and in a sense they were right to see in Dundas their arch-enemy, the enemy of idealism, of principle in politics—and of cant. They might well shout "We have killed the fox!" The resolutions that charged

HENRY DUNDAS

him with peculation, violation of the law and a breach of duty were carried only by the Speaker's casting vote: but they went through partly from the vehemence of Wilberforce, himself originally a Dundas man before he became a "Saint", and of Sidmouth (Addington), Dundas's bitterest enemy. That he had enemies the division made clear. In justifying his conduct subsequently, Wilberforce claimed that the fault he found in Melville was merely in acting "foolishly", that he was really "a fine warm-hearted fellow": but history has come uncritically to accept Wilberforce's view that it was his connexion with Dundas that was Pitt's greatest misfortune. Certainly Pitt was broken by the blow. Dundas was acquitted at the impeachment, the last in British history. There was no evidence provided to prove that he had been either personally corrupt or personally a beneficiary from public funds. He had used those funds, avowedly and on Pitt's authority, to steady the currency in the panic of 1797. His protégé, Alexander Trotter, a voter in Midlothian, had certainly been culpable as Paymaster, and had used public funds for private speculation, and to buy an estate. Dundas was acquitted: but, as always, the scars remain. As Charlotte Nugent wrote to Admiral Cornwallis during the trial, "His situation puts me in mind of Cardinal Wolsey. He is undone by his ambition . . .".

It was not quite true, but near enough. His fall proved complete. Like many an old man, he always had hopes of being recalled to office; amid all the denials, the dreams died slowly and reluctantly. The Bishop of Lichfield described him in 1810, the year before his death, as "older, and, I thought, like all un-placed statesmen, feeling the lack of former consequence". Like them, too, he who had built up a party strength counselled his son against being a party man. His fall was not a personal, yet it was a political, disaster for his cause.

> His impeachment, (says Cockburn), "did more to emancipate Scotland than even the exclusion of his party from power . . . the progress of independence was materially advanced . . . Our little great men felt the precariousness of their power . . . the mainspring of the Scotch pro-consular system was weakened.[9]

It is easy to pile up the indictment against Dundas, for he was not a heroic figure; there was nothing of the idealist in him. If he was a liberal on a few issues in the early years, he was no campaigner for fugitive causes. In Wraxall's phrase, he thought a speculative tenet to be "undeserving of contention".[10] He was not fertile in ideas, least of all political or social ideas. Although a gifted speaker, his literary equipment was thin, his spelling and grammar were feeble, his tastes were crude. As Lockhart put it, a trifle too elegantly, "he was always happy to drink his bottle of port with any worthy man of any party". The *Rolliad*, a harsher critic, charged him in 1785 as lacking in modesty and continence:

> What various tastes divide the fickle town!
> One likes the fair, and one admires the brown,
> The stately, Queensb'ry; Hinchinbrook the small;
> Thurlow loves servant maids; Dundas loves all.

[9] Henry Cockburn, *Memorials of his Time* (Edinburgh, 1856), pp. 216-17.

[10] *Memoirs*, Vol. 3 (London 1884), p. 67.

HENRY DUNDAS

There was a streak of coarseness, the penalty of his strength. For his talents were administrative and manipulative. He believed in government—he wished well, as he put it in 1781, to the Government of the country "in whosoever hands". He was ready to serve it, because government was something manufactured, a matter in the eighteenth century more of contrivance than conviction. In service of country, done assiduously and competently, lay satisfaction and promotion of self: these were, as they are apt to be for most politicians in all ages, causes hard to separate from each other. This is not a hostile judgment if we seek to judge him by the standards of his day. If Pitt was nobler, he could be uncharitable, and he never easily relaxed his own tight, if dedicated, grip on power; Wilberforce was curiously blind on many issues; Fox was quixotic and unreliable; not everything was gold that glittered in Burke. Dundas's was not a noble, or a flexible, mind, but it was realistic; if it could not recognise the force of ideas, it saw quickly to the kernel of political and military facts. If he did nothing to reform the system of government, he operated it deftly and without harshness. Dundas was a pluralist, but a Unionist; he was coarse, but he had a Walpolian vitality, gusto and sense. He was not in politics for his health: but he rendered some service to both his countries.

R. J. White

THE YOUNGER PITT
The Great Solitary[1]

He has patronised no science, he has raised no man of genius from obscurity; he counts no one prime work of God among his friends. From the same source he has no attachment to female society, no fondness for children, no perceptions of beauty in natural scenery; but he is fond of convivial indulgences, of that stimulation which, keeping up the glow of self-importance and the sense of internal power, gives feelings without the mediation of ideas.

Thus, in the year 1800, one man of genius at the age of twenty-eight wrote of another man of genius who was forty-one. Coleridge's *Character of Mr Pitt* appeared in *The Morning Post*, and it struck the note that was to resound at the mention of "Pitt-and-port" for a hundred years, whenever a Whig or a Radical writer took pen in hand to do injustice to the subject. Even in the middle of the twentieth century, after the notably sympathetic studies by Lord Rosebery and Holland Rose, Pitt remains the great solitary among English statesmen—a

[1] [Copyright © R. J. White. Originally published in *History Today*, II (1952), pp. 696-702.]

12. 1798. Fox as a minister of the Directory, standing on the royal arms.

13. 1804. Hawkesbury, Addington, and St Vincent under attack. Fox is held up by Buckingham and his brother, Grenville, and hits Addington in the eye with his spray of shot. Pitt has Dundas behind him and Canning on the steps below him, armed with "killing detections". Grey is the bowman beneath Pitt's left foot. Windham brandishes spear and shield on the right, while Tierney encourages Sheridan and Erskine to climb the ladder to the government.

THE YOUNGER PITT   105

cold, lofty, monumental figure, seeming to stare down
the forces of domestic malice and foreign enmity as if
they were personal affronts to his severe and disdainful
spirit. The best-known portraits of the man tell the same
tale, whether we look at Gainsborough's elegant render-
ing of the youthful Chancellor of the Exchequer or at
Hoppner's dark portrait, executed when Pitt was forty-
seven, of the worn and weary man within a year of his
death. Even in Hickel's picture of Pitt addressing the
House of Commons, the Prime Minister stands out from
his followers like a solitary crow among a covey of
partridges. This air of solitude is no illusion conceived by
posterity; and our attempts to modify it are as mistaken
as they are futile. Better far to face the fact, and to try to
fathom its significance. The truth is that Pitt's solitude
was the solitude of superiority, of a transcendent greatness of ability and character—no easy admission in an
age that likes to describe itself as one of the Common
Man, an age that would prefer to believe that greatness
is a product of circumstances, and those chiefly economic.
Today, the notion that the greatness of a great man does
honour to our common human nature appears to have
escaped us.

William Pitt was the son of a great father, William
Pitt, the first Earl of Chatham. He was born in 1759, the
year of his father's crowning glory, when it was said that
Englishmen opened their newspapers every morning to
read of the latest triumph of their country's arms. Men
attributed these victories over the ancient enemy to the
inspiring leadership of The Great Commoner, the man
with the face of an eagle and the heart of a lion. Yet, of all

P.P.—H

the achievements of Pitt the Elder, one of the most important for his country was the siring and rearing of Pitt the Younger. When the young man made his maiden speech in the House of Commons, Edmund Burke exclaimed: "He is not a chip of the old block; it is the old block itself." This was true. Young William's nose turned up, whereas his father's had turned down; his genius lay in the management of finance rather than in the wielding of a war-machine; his temper was far more cold than choleric. But he inherited his father's wide-ranging grasp of big issues, his capacity to exercise political power as if it were a limb of his own body, his utterly single-minded devotion to an ideal that contained within its broad scope the purposes of a whole generation of men. Between them, the Pitts raised the tone of eighteenth-century public life in England to no less a degree than John Wesley raised the tone of private life. The age was a corrupt one: the *ancien régime* throughout contemporary Europe was marked by personal greed, habitual graft, and cheerful coarseness of fibre in everything concerning the public service. Whatever may be said for the wisdom of Walpole—and there is much that can be said—it remains true that he found political morality at a very low ebb and left it where he found it. To the Pitts we owe the change that occurred. It was this, as much as the husbanding of England's material resources and the scientific organisation of public finance, that enabled England to meet and defeat the revolutionary tyranny of the Jacobins, the Directory, and Napoleon. Years after Chatham's death, Englishmen believed that the affairs of their country would be in safe hands so long as they were

THE YOUNGER PITT
107

entrusted to the care of his son. That moral probity which had somehow become synonymous with the name of Pitt was the substantial basis of his authority. Nor is this judgment impaired by the indubitable fact that Pitt the Younger was among the most ambitious and skilfully Machiavellian of the ministers who have held power in England.

Pitt loved power with the consuming passion that excludes all other appetites. His personal rectitude, his abstention from almost all forms of self-indulgence which engage the mind and senses of ordinary humanity— these were sacrifices made for the sake of whole-time absorption in his master-passion: politics. He was, as Coleridge rather unkindly put it, "a young man whose feet had never wandered, whose very eye had never turned to the right or to the left, whose whole track had been as curveless as the motion of a fascinated reptile!" Thus Coleridge accounts for his solitude: "It was a young man whose heart was solitary, because he had existed always amid objects of futurity . . ." To Pitt futurity meant the government of England by himself; the good government of England, certainly, but always by Pitt. He never said, as his father had said: "I know that I can save this country, and that no one else can." Instead, he declared: "I place much dependence upon my new colleagues; I place still more dependence on myself." He could depend upon himself because he knew himself; he knew what he wanted. Moreover, he knew how to get what he wanted: knew exactly what kind of minister the English people would trust, what interests he must cherish, what aspirations must be sacrificed—and at what *point* they must be sacrificed—if his authority was to be maintained. On this last point, his great rival, Charles James Fox, is our best authority. "He is very civil and obliging, profuse of compliments in public", Fox wrote of his young friend: "but he has more than once taken a line that has alarmed me, especially when he dissuaded against going into any inquiries that might produce heats and differences . . ."

Fox, the man of generous enthusiasm, the great tribune of opposition, had laid his finger on the truth about Pitt. Pitt would never die, politically speaking, for a principle. Every measure that he produced was designed to avoid affront to established interests, to avoid "heats and differences". There was to be parliamentary reform with generous compensation for the owners of disfranchised boroughs; the East India Company was to be "nationalised" without injury to the Directors; the slave-trade was to be abolished without loss to the slavers; Irish Union was to be achieved without injury to the Protestant ascendancy. If these things could only be done by engendering "heats and differences", Pitt preferred that they should not be done at all. Thus, both parliamentary reform and the abolition of the slave-trade had to await the coming of other days and other men. With an imperious off-handedness that infuriated not only his enemies but many of his friends, Pitt was always prepared to withdraw an offending measure and go on to something else. If politics is the art of the possible, Pitt was its most accomplished master. But it is the pursuit of the impossible, or at least the perilous and difficult, that wins the hearts and imaginations of men.

THE YOUNGER PITT

Pitt's almost instinctive mastery of parliamentary tactics was never exhibited with greater brilliance than during the three years that intervened between his election to Parliament and his assumption of the office of Prime Minister. In those three years—the shortest time for such a journey on record—he played a waiting game with such skill and patience, that Fox and his friends damned themselves with a thoroughness that consigned them for more than twenty years to the political wilderness. Given enough rope, Pitt would seem to have argued, Fox would hang himself. And that is what he did. By going into coalition with Lord North, the man who for more than twelve years had been the principal target of his attack as the head and front of royal misgovernment, Fox destroyed his own public character as no mere party rival could have done. Moreover, the Coalition brought to a head all that the English people had grown to detest in parliamentary life for half a century. That "unnatural alliance" seemed to epitomise the jobbery, corruption, intrigue, and factiousness of the *ancien régime*. The young man who came to power over its dead body—a young man bearing the honoured name of Pitt—was readily associated with all the hopes of an outraged nation looking for a saviour. That nation did not put Pitt into power by the unimpeded action of its will as expressed through the ballot-box. The King called Pitt to office, and kept him there for many months in defiance of the crowded and frantic ranks of the opposition. Even when an election was held, in 1784, it was as carefully managed by the King and his Treasury as any election of the century. But it was still true, as a contemporary observed, that "the Public, and the Public only, enabled Pitt to defeat the powerful phalanx drawn up against him". It was to be the public, largely unenfranchised though it was, that kept Pitt in power with scarcely a break for the next twenty years.

On the ruins of the Fox-North Coalition, on the confidence of George III, on the interests of a growing business community, and on the support of an unenfranchised people, Pitt built the great political connexion that was to maintain him for so long. "Connexion" is a better word than "Party" to describe the forces that upheld his authority. Neither the Whig nor the Tory label really fits him or the forces that were behind him. He was always a Whig in that he stood for responsible ministerial government in the tradition of the Glorious Revolution: but then, so were the Tories. Perhaps his Whiggery comes out more strongly in his devotion to the interests of the City of London and the commercial community in general. Disraeli and Cobbett alike were to denounce him for opening too wide the door that led from the counting-house to the House of Lords. Retrospectively, however, he appears a Tory, the founder of the great anti-Jacobin party which was to rule England in the age of Liverpool and Castlereagh. In his relations with George III he was neither Whig nor Tory, but the trusted intermediary between King and Parliament in a delicately balanced system of constitutional government. George III soon learned, however, that the young man who had saved him from Fox was no latter-day Lord North. Pitt had first his name in Parliament by his ardent participation in the typically Whig activity of

THE YOUNGER PITT

striving to limit the royal influence in politics by "Economical Reform". He was not prepared to rule England either for or against the King, only to rule with the King. He controlled his Cabinet like a modern Prime Minister, standing between his colleagues and the royal master, personally representing the royal master to them and to Parliament. George III knew that he could not dispense with Pitt; and Pitt knew that he must always persuade the King that his policy was in accordance with the best intentions of a patriotic monarch. His management of King George's well-intentioned, but often perverse, will was superb. Out of this situation—the King's necessities and his own indispensability—he forged something recognisably like our modern system of Cabinet government. The keynote of the whole was discipline. It was because Pitt's public life was his only life, because he was prepared to be the King's first minister twenty-four hours a day, to see to everything himself and to maintain a god-like omniscience and ubiquity, that he was able to make the greatest contribution of any single man to Cabinet government as we see it today.

It was during the dangerous years after 1789 that the concentration of authority in the person of the Prime Minister became most obvious. War, the menace of revolutionary attack upon national institutions, the threat of invasion in alliance with a fifth column at home: these things, as we know well enough, demand the concentration of power in the hands of those who are most capable of using it with the necessary speed, secrecy, and effect. For more than ten years, Pitt stood at the heart of an England beset by mortal danger. Yet, unlike

Chatham and Churchill, he was not one to revel in danger; indeed, he was for long accused of undue complacency. It could not be said of him, as it was said of Burke, that, when he spoke of the French Revolution, his face assumed "the expression of a man who is going to defend himself against murderers". He had never shared the ignorant animosity of Englishmen towards France and the French. "To suppose that any nation can be unalterably the enemy of another is weak and childish", he told the House of Commons in 1787, when his opponents attacked the Eden Treaty which was designed to promote freer commercial intercourse with our "traditional enemy". Such a notion, he went on, "has its foundation neither in the experience of nations nor in the history of man. It is a libel on the constitution of political societies and supposes the existence of diabolical malice in the original frame of man".

Pitt seems to have taken little stock in the doctrine of original sin as applied to whole nations; and he was never greatly impressed by what publicists call "the logic of events" or by any other form of historical determinism. To him, France was a good customer for English textiles and an exporter of excellent wines. As a disciple of Adam Smith and a believer in the theory of comparative costs, he wished to promote a freer exchange between the two countries in those commodities which they could produce best and most cheaply. France, moreover, was an exporter of excellent ideas. The teaching of Adam Smith owed much to the French Physiocrats; intellectual free trade between the two peoples was something that Pitt had learnt to prize from experience.

THE YOUNGER PITT

True, he was a little alarmed when, on the eve of the Revolution, M. Necker seemed likely to restore France's financial stability and thus enable her to rival England in the trade of the East: but it is as well to remember that France was at that time a vastly more populous and potentially more wealthy country than England, and much given to aggression at English expense. There was in Pitt's England a good deal of rancour against France for her part in assisting the revolt of the American colonies. Many were ready to see, in the French Revolution, the hand of vengeance falling upon the formenter of rebellion. Pitt was wiser. He shared the more enlightened view of those who saw in the events of 1789 the prospect of constitutional government in France, the kind of government that might lend a stable and pacific character to her policy. The trouble with French foreign policies under the *ancien régime* had been their recklessness, malice, and unpredictability. With a constitutional system answerable to the needs of the nation, there would be hope of peace and friendship. It was the attitude of Dr Price, not of Burke; and if it was an illusion, it was a generous one. The charge against Pitt, should a charge be brought, cannot be that of Francophobia. Up to the last possible moment, he sought friendship with France, and only went to war against the Revolution after it had struck the first blow. Then he saw it as a war for national survival against an arrogant nationalism which threatened to overturn the balance of power in Europe, and to hold a pistol to the head of England by conquest of the Low Countries.

As for the Jacobins at home, Pitt allowed them no

mercy; his name has always been associated with the stern policy of repression which became a Tory tradition down to the year of Peterloo, and even beyond. "They thought they were imitating Mr Pitt, because they mistook disorganisation for sedition," wrote Disraeli of the Tories of Lord Liverpool's government, at the safe distance of a quarter of a century. For many years, no epithet was too venomous among English Radicals for "that bloody-handed tool of tyranny, William Pitt". He was accused of inventing revolutionary plots, in order to repress more savagely the champions of reform and make his own tenure of office appear indispensable. The severity of his measures cannot be denied: but the nature of the problem with which they were intended to deal has often been misunderstood. The question is not whether there really existed in England a widespread revolutionary conspiracy. Pitt was faced with something far more dangerous because far less susceptible of detection. He knew—and Lord Liverpool knew, and said—that revolutions are not made: they happen. It was not the multitude that was dangerous; nor even the few bold and fanatical agitators. At a time of national crisis and economic distress, the peril lay in the ubiquity of reformist associations, linked by "correspondence" and at the mercy of unscrupulous men; in the assumption of quasi-sovereign pretensions by "Conventions", claiming the status of "shadow-parliaments"; in the snowball process by which multifarious innocent activities could accumulate the weight of an avalanche.

Finally, we should remember that Pitt and his generation had seen unplanned revolution blaze up to a climax

THE YOUNGER PITT 115

which stopped short of total catastrophe thanks only to the courage displayed by the King, Alderman John Wilkes, and certain other gentlemen of the City of London. No one who had lived through the Gordon Riots of 1780 was likely to underestimate the dangers of unpremeditated revolution. A crazy Peer, a popular war-cry—it happened to be the old one, "No Popery!"— a general emergence of the slum and cellar population; and London was in flames, and at the mercy of a roaring, drunken, looting populace for six dreadful days and nights. Long before the revolution in Paris, Europe had come to regard London as the natural home of mob-violence. The line between mob-violence and revolution is easier to draw after the event than by the light of a burning capital. In the very near background of every English statesman down to 1820 was a memory of the events of June, 1780. To them, the storming of the Bastille and the September Massacres had an apparent English ancestry.

Pitt fought the war with France on two fronts— "malice domestic" was, or seemed to be, as menacing as "foreign levy"; until, with the rise of Napoleon Bonaparte, the threat to national survival and the likelihood of imminent invasion served to drive all but a handful of the most hardened Francophiles into the solidarity of patriotic endeavour. Then it was that the work of the Pitts, father and son, bore fruit in the devotion and sacrifice of a regenerated people. In particular, the Younger Pitt's great financial reforms, his pacification of the Empire, and his nourishment of trade and industry, proved their worth by helping England to build up the war-chest that was to finance coalition after coalition until the hour of victory. "Pitt's Gold" became a legend among England's allies, and an excuse for her thwarted enemies. Pitt made mistakes; he was not, like his father, a genius of war. But, even when he died, in the dark hour of Ulm and Austerlitz, his steadfast courage and endless resourcefulness had already put his country on the path to victory. Those who came after him were not, for the most part, big enough to wear his mantle: but the very cut and rig of the garment supported them in their flounderings upon the tide that swept forward to Salamanca, Leipzig, and the final field of Waterloo. As he lay dying in the dark January days of 1806, Pitt cried out in agony upon the situation of his country: but it was he, and he alone, who had taught England to save herself by her exertions and to save Europe by her example.

The stature of the great solitary has grown with time. The wars and revolutions of the twentieth century have taught us that Pitt was not a monster, but a giant. If he lacks charm, it is because his life was all public; he looms like an institution rather than a creature of our flesh and blood. Even on his death-bed, he is said to have cried not upon the mercy of God but upon the House of Commons. "Hear—hear!" were the words that escaped his lips in his last delirium. What he believed about man's final purpose and destiny he kept to himself, as he kept so much else. As his dear friend, William Wilberforce, tells us, Pitt always said less on these subjects than he thought. A true son of his age, he despised "enthusiasm", contenting himself with the formal observance of the rites and consolations of the established Church. Yet, somewhere

THE YOUNGER PITT

within that spare and frigid form, there lived the invincible peace of a quiet spirit.

God bless you, my dear Pitt, and carry you through all your difficulties (Wilberforce once wrote to him). You may reckon yourself most fortunate in that cheerfulness of mind which enables you to throw off your load for a few hours and rest yourself. I fancy it must be this which, when I am with you, prevents my considering you as an object of compassion tho' Prime Minister of England. . . .

M. G. Brock

GEORGE CANNING[1]

Canning became prime minister in April 1827 and died in the following August. It took him the greater part of these four months to form his government, and the task had not been completed at his death. Seen from one angle, his premiership was the brief and tragic climax of a long struggle for power: from another it was an attempt by a statesman of great political prescience to save the unreformed Parliament and system of government.

> There has been but one man for many years past, (Greville wrote during the reform agitation), able to arrest this torrent, and that was Canning; and him the Tories—idiots that they were, and never discovering that he was their best friend—hunted to death with their besotted and ignorant hostility.

There is substance in Greville's remark. Canning possessed unique qualifications for saving the old order, but few of the members of that order regarded him as a

---

[1] [Copyright © M. G. Brock. Originally published in *History Today*, I (Aug. 1951), pp. 33-40.] Quotations from unpublished MSS. are made by kind permission of the Right Hon. The Earl of Harrowby (Harrowby MSS.), Viscount Hardinge, M.B.E. (Hardinge MSS., South Park), and the Council of Nottingham University (Portland MSS.).

GEORGE CANNING

saviour. The reasons for this distrust lay deep in his past.

Pitt, to whom Canning owed all his early promotion, referred to his protégé's "ungovernable ambition". Unlike Disraeli, Canning was never able to conceal his impatience to reach the top of the greasy pole. At various times in the eighteen-fifties Disraeli offered to surrender the party leadership in the Commons to Gladstone, Palmerston, and Graham. Canning, at a comparable period in his career, was demanding a higher place than even his splendid talents merited. In 1809, while still under forty, he refused to serve under Perceval, who had led the Commons in the previous government and was nearly eight years his senior. Three years later he declined the Foreign Office because the leadership of the House was not coupled with it. These inordinate demands, which kept him out of office during the years of victory, were combined with dubious manoeuvres. When Pitt resigned in 1801, he determined to give his successor Addington a fair run, and pressed his colleagues to do the same; Canning refused, and made bitter enemies of the Addingtonians. In 1807, though a supporter of Catholic emancipation, Canning was part-author of a highly successful dissolution on the "No Popery" cry. Throughout the spring of 1809, while still a member of Portland's moribund cabinet, he angled for the co-operation of the Whig opposition, expecting that the King would make him Portland's successor. "The real truth is", Richard Ryder wrote to Harrowby, "that he considers politics as a game and has no idea of any regard to principle interfering with his object of getting into power".[2] And

[2] Harrowby MSS.: transcript: original in family shorthand-cypher.

this was the opinion of a sympathetic observer who, like Canning, belonged to Pitt's personal following.

Although towards the end of his life Canning acquired more circumspection and restraint, he never had complete command over his feelings and temper. His emotions were easily roused even by the standards of his own day, and his tears, it is said, "flowed at Chalmers' sermons or at the recollection of his own speeches". In debate it was not difficult to enrage him, and after his death Wellington gave Greville the following account of his behaviour in Cabinet:

> Any difference of opinion or dissent from his views threw him into ungovernable rage, and on such occasions he flew out with a violence which, the D. said, had often compelled him to be silent that he might not be involved in bitter personal altercation.

He could no more control his wit than his anger. Most of his best jokes were made against those whose help he would some day need. It was not wise to suggest that Charles Wynn, who had a piping voice, should be addressed as "Mr Squeaker", if elevated to the Chair, since Wynn was a member of the powerful Grenville clan. It was injudicious to lampoon Addington's promotion of his brother Hiley and brother-in-law, Bragge Bathurst:

> How blest, how firm the Statesman stands
> (Him no low intrigue can move),
> Circled by faithful kindred bands
> And propped by fond fraternal love,
> When his speeches hobble vilely,
> What "Hear him's" burst from brother Hiley;
> When his faltering periods lag,
> Hark to the cheers of Brother Bragge.

14. 1808. Pitt drops his mantle towards Canning, while Hawkesbury and Castlereagh also reach up for it. Under Fox's cloak, Grenville has his cardinal's hat blown off, Grey his republican bonnet. In the far distance, Napoleon is also losing his hat.

15. 1827. George IV with his newly chosen Prime Minister, Canning. Wellington and Eldon are among those lost in the Sea of Pride.

GEORGE CANNING

If the Bathursts and Addingtons were ridiculous, they were also influential. But Canning was an Irishman, and could not help letting fly. Even when his wit did not wound, it gave him a dangerous reputation for flippancy, of being "a light, jesting, paragraph-making man". By the time he fought his duel with Castlereagh, Canning had gained a reputation for several characteristics disastrous in British politics—derisive wit, voracious ambition, and a love of intrigue.

The distrust which Canning faced when he became premier was not therefore due solely to his being "the son of an actress".[3] It had been aroused by his defects and mistakes at least as much as by his origins. The unreformed Parliament, as its apologists boasted, gave a flying start to talented young men, even if they had been born outside the charmed circle. Many of the leading Tories of Canning's day—Croker, Herries, and Lyndhurst, for instance—were of relatively humble birth. Canning's Eton reputation gained him an early introduction to Pitt. The Prime Minister secured his unopposed return for a rotten borough at the age of twenty-three, appointed him Under-Secretary for Foreign Affairs two years later, helped to make a wealthy match for him, and gave him a Privy Councillorship when he was thirty. The brilliant young men without connexions of Disraeli's generation were less fortunate: there were no nomination boroughs for them.

---

[3] When Canning was a year old, his father died, and his mother, Mary Anne, tried to make her living on the stage without much success. In 1827 Grey thought Canning, as the "son of an actress", "*de facto* incapacitated from being premier."

P.P.—I

Nevertheless, there were limits to the patricians' willingness to admit outsiders to their ranks. It was one thing to enlist the aid of a "lackland" adventurer, another to serve under him. The deplorable sneers at Canning's government made by those born in the purple did not derive merely from snobbery and outraged pride. Behind them lay the belief that Canning and his like, who were not themselves men of substantial property, would not serve the interests of the great proprietors faithfully. When Canning's followers were searching for a Prime Minister after his death, Lord George Bentinck wrote to the Duke of Portland:

> Huskisson holds the opinion that the country requires that a man of rank, property and consideration should be at the Head of the Administration ... (his) opinion and I think that of the World is that were a man of your consideration and moderate Principles at the Head of Affairs ... the Govt. would be pretty secure.[4]

The Duke of Portland had never taken a leading, or even an active, part in politics: but it may well be that his "rank, property and consideration" would have proved weightier assets in the premiership than all Canning's genius.

In 1822 these mistakes and disabilities determined Canning to quit politics. Despairing of his prospects, he accepted the Governor-Generalship of India, and he was taking leave of his constituents at Liverpool when Castlereagh's suicide left the Foreign Office vacant for him. His survival in the front rank therefore owed

[4] Portland MSS.

GEORGE CANNING

something to chance: but in the main it was due to an array of talents seldom equalled in British public life. He possessed a complete equipment for the parliamentary eloquence most admired in his day. After Fox's death he had no rival as an orator, though most hearers thought him a little theatrical and consequently sometimes wanting in the power to convince the House of his sincerity. "Canning's ... speeches excellent", Wilberforce noted in his journal in 1811, "but not like Pitt's; rather exciting admiration than calling forth sympathy". No one denied, however, their immense effectiveness. Allied to an open and generous disposition which his outbursts of temper never destroyed, they gave him complete command of the House, which he was said to rule "as Alexander ruled Bucephalus".

He was equally effective in his department. "Canning, I think", said Wellington, "was readier at writing than even at speaking; I never in my life knew so great a master of his pen". This facility was reinforced by great powers of hard work and concentration. Dudley, who succeeded Canning as Foreign Secretary, wrote: "His habits of industry must appear quite incredible to those who did not know him."

> He could not bear to dictate, (one of his secretaries told Greville), because nobody could write fast enough for him; but on one occasion, when he had the gout in his hand and could not write, he stood by the fire and dictated at the same time a despatch on Greek affairs to George Bentinck and one on South American politics to Howard de Walden, each writing as fast as he could, while he turned from one to the other without hesitation or embarrassment.

P.P.—I*

Nor was he merely a man of words. His seizure of the Danish fleet in 1807, and the recognition of the revolted Spanish colonies, show his decision and tenacity in action. In every sphere he displayed the same peerless rapidity of mind.

When he became Foreign Secretary in 1822, he faced the King's bitter hostility for his part in the affair of Queen Caroline's trial, and he was without an ally in the Cabinet. The King was quickly won round by adroit courtiership. Canning appointed Lord Francis Conyngham, the royal mistress's son, his under-secretary, and also, if Greville may be believed, secured an appointment in Buenos Aires for a subject whose continued presence in England would have been inconvenient to his sovereign. But these personal services were only part of the story: George IV longed for popularity, and Canning could give it to him. There had been violent royal opposition to recognising the revolted Spanish colonies, but, in Greville's words,

> when the King found that none of the evils predicted of this measure had come to pass, and how it raised the reputation of his Minister, he liked it very well, and Canning dexterously gave him all the praise of it, so that he soon fancied it had originated with himself, and became equally satisfied with himself and with Canning.

In the Cabinet Canning established an alliance with the Prime Minister, whose friend he had been at Christ Church. Liverpool, though opposed to him on the great political question of the day, Catholic emancipation, soon enraged the "Protestant" wing of the Cabinet by siding with him regularly. "The Duke said Ld. Liverpool had

GEORGE CANNING 125

really no opinion of his own," Mrs Arbuthnot noted in February 1824; "that he was completely under the dominion of Canning . . . Mr Peel said that Ld. Liverpool's meanness and subjection to Canning was beyond expression contemptible and disgusting."

More remarkable than either of these victories was the speed with which Canning won the support of commercial circles, and of the educated public in general, for his foreign policy. From 1812 to 1822 he had been member for Liverpool, and he knew far more about mercantile opinion than his predecessor or any of his colleagues. He was the first Foreign Secretary to explain his policy in platform speeches. In 1824 a Whig paper, the *Morning Herald*, thought "that no minister, since the Revolution, excepting only the great Lord Chatham, has acquired the same national popularity which is at this moment possessed by Mr Canning". Within three years of joining the Government, Canning had won the confidence and support of the King, the Prime Minister, and the great majority of the public.

These accomplishments would not themselves prove Greville to have been right in suggesting that Canning was the Tories' best friend, who could have arrested the reform torrent had he lived. The outline of Canning's qualities given above is compatible with the view of his detractors that he was merely an unprincipled adventurer of great abilities and ambition, whose mind, whether he was acting as courtier or demagogue, worked quicker than other men's. But this view cannot be supported. From the time he enlisted with Pitt, Canning adhered to certain political principles with complete consistency.

"Jacobinism", wrote Charles Bagot, "*that* is the antagonist of Canning." The periodical which he inspired in his youth was well named "The Anti-Jacobin". His career, like that of every statesman of his time, was passed in the shadow of the French revolution. Like Eldon and Wellington he was the undeviating foe of revolutionary ideas. Like them he opposed parliamentary reform to the end, and denounced "pure democracy" and a House of Commons that should be "a direct effectual representative of the people". But unlike them, he did not think these negatives enough. He had grasped in part, as they had not, the significance of the commercial and industrial changes of his day.

Canning realised that, with the revolution and war no more than a memory, concessions had become essential. The fear of a revolutionary upheaval, which had united the propertied classes in resisting all change, was fading. If the unreformed Parliament did nothing to meet the reasonable demands of merchants and manufacturers, they would not tolerate it long. "They who resist indiscriminately all improvements as innovations", he told the Commons, "may find themselves compelled at last to submit to innovations although they are not improvements." It requires artistry to kindle enthusiasm for a programme of judicious concessions, and Canning was a considerable artist. "He flashed such a light around the constitution", said Coleridge, "that it was difficult to see the ruins of the fabric through it." Canning boasted that the arguments for reform of Parliament rested solely on electoral theory, and that there were no "practical grievances" against the existing system. The boast

GEORGE CANNING   127

seemed largely justified: after five years of Canning at the Foreign Office and Huskisson at the Board of Trade, the grievances found no more than faint utterance. During Canning's premiership Grey confessed that parliamentary reform had little hold upon the country.

This liberal brand of Toryism, which re-established Canning's prestige with the public, only increased his colleague's hostility. To long-standing personal distrust of him was now added a belief that his craving for popular applause would lead him into dangerous concessions. Canning was fully equipped by his abilities and past to frame a policy that would keep his party in power, but he was not equipped to make them adopt it. Liverpool had a stroke in February 1827 and eight weeks of manoeuvring for the premiership followed. The high Tories played their cards badly, giving the King the impression that they were trying to dictate to him. In the end he commissioned Canning to form a government. The choice was no mere caprice: probably, with Canning on his flank, no other statesman would have made the attempt. Six Cabinet ministers, including Wellington and Peel, refused to serve under Canning and resigned, Wellington even throwing up the command of the army as well as his Cabinet post. There were over forty resignations in all from the government and royal household. The old Tory party of Pitt and Liverpool was broken beyond repair.

It would be a mistake to attribute this secession entirely to personal distrust of Canning and dislike of his methods. The quarrel went deeper. In 1827 Canning was in rather the same position as Peel in 1845, or Joseph

Chamberlain in 1903. All three, at those dates, belonged to governments which had long been in the ascendant; in all three cases the ascendancy had been due chiefly to alarm; in all three the alarm had grown faint. By 1827 Jacobinism seemed a distant danger; by 1845 Peel's "great Conservative party" no longer feared the Radicals; by 1903 there seemed little likelihood that the Liberals would carry home rule. In each case the party's cohesion had been due to fear, and in each, as fear diminished, the rifts appeared. All three statesmen concerned were turning towards new policies, which might have won their parties new support—Canning to liberalism, Peel to Cobdenism, Chamberlain to tariff reform. To the less forward-looking members of those parties, all three seemed more dangerous than the opposition. None of them succeeded in winning the whole party round, and two of them, of whom Canning was one, were killed by the effort to do so.

From 1822 to 1827, in 1845 and 1846, and from 1903 to 1905, the crucial struggle for power was fought out, not between the parties, but within the party forming the government. Liverpool's Cabinet were thoroughly used to finding their worst enemies on their own side of the House. "The real opposition of the present day", wrote Palmerston in 1826, "sit behind the Treasury Bench." Canning's elevation to the premiership transferred this battle into the open, but did not decide it. During the short time that he faced the Commons as premier, his enemies avoided a trial of strength. It is impossible, therefore, to say whether his government would have stood had he lived. The forces in the Commons were

GEORGE CANNING 129

evenly matched. He had the crown's influence, his personal following, most of the Whigs, and a good deal of independent support. His opponents included the ultra Tories, most of the nominees of the great borough owners, and a small section of the Whigs. In the Lords he was weaker, and there his opponents, led by Wellington, passed a wrecking amendment to his Corn Bill by four votes.

Whichever side wins, a battle in the party forming the government must benefit the opposition. In 1830, as in 1846 and 1905, the opposition were the great gainers. It is difficult to believe that, had Canning lived, this result would have been affected. In any case Canning's death, unlike Peel's, was no sudden accident. His health had long since shown signs of failing. In January 1824 he was not expected by Liverpool to "last many sessions in the H. of Commons". In September 1825 Sir Walter Scott was shocked by his appearance. Only a year after his return to office Canning wrote to a friend: "The two functions of For. Sec. and Leader of the H. of C. are too much for any man—and ought not to be united; though I of course would rather die under them than separate them." He needed to hold both posts to establish his pre-eminence, and the double burden wore him out. When he became Prime Minister he was a dying man, drugging himself with laudanum.

Nor would a government retaining power by Whig support have represented success for Canning's plans. Its continuance could not have cancelled the effect of the secession of his Tory colleagues. He had not converted his party to accept his leadership and his ideas. This failure was final, and immensely disruptive. His attempt to lead and save the Tories had weakened them and increased their feuds. His legacy, as Wellington rightly said, was a "divided government party".

Transcending all other causes of this failure was the fact that in 1827 the Tories felt safe. They would only accept Canning and Canning's policy of concession in the face of obvious danger, and in 1827 the danger, though great, was not apparent. To succeed, Canning had to persuade the party that only he could save them. Those who seceded from his government believed the exact reverse of this.

> "Whatever may happen", Wellington wrote to Hardinge the day after Canning's death, "the 'Child and Champion' of Radicalism (under the Mask of a Protector of the Rights of the Crown) is gone. Those who remain cannot assume that mask; and have it not in their Power to do a tithe of the Mischief which he could and would have done. I think his death has been so far premature as that neither had the King felt the Inconvenience of the step he took in April, nor are the publick yet aware of the false pretences on which the Govt. was founded. . . .
>
> Mr. Canning's death therefore will not do all the good it might have done at a later period. But it is still a great publick advantage."[5]

Most of the Tory aristocracy would have agreed with this view. At first Canning hoped to defy these magnates. When Croker wrote to him, pointing out how many votes they controlled in the Commons, he replied:

> Am I to understand, then, that you consider the King as completely in the hands of the Tory aristocracy as . . .

[5] Hardinge MSS.

George II was in the hands of the Whigs? If so, George III reigned, and Mr. Pitt . . . administered the Government in vain.

I have a better opinion of the real vigour of the Crown when it chooses to put forth its own strength, and I am not without some reliance on the body of the people.

But Croker was uncomfortably near the truth. The borough owners held the key position, as Canning recognised in his final despairing prophecy.

"We are on the brink", he said, a few weeks before his death, "of a great struggle between property and population. Such a struggle is only to be averted by the mildest and most liberal legislation. . . . If the policy of the Newcastles and Northumberlands is to prevail, that struggle cannot be staved off much longer."

A large part of the unreformed Parliament was in the hands of the Newcastles and Northumberlands, and they would not be warned. With Canning dead the system crumbled quickly. The Tories salvaged a good deal from the reform torrent, but not the nomination boroughs. Canning, as Greville suggested, had been the borough owners' last chance.

NOTES ON ILLUSTRATION

The numbers in brackets are those of the British Museum *Catalogue of Political and Personal Satires*, from which further information may be obtained.

1. *John Wilkes Esqr*. Hogarth. (4050) It was said that nearly four thousand copies of this etching were produced in a few weeks. For no. 17 and no. 45 of the *North Briton*, see above, pp. 9, 51.

2. *The Captive Prince*. Author unknown. (5979) North's resignation left the unhappy King with no alternative but a Rockingham ministry committed to curb what they maintained had been his excessive influence. Fox was reported to have said that "this Revolution which he brought about was the greatest for England that ever was; that excepting in the mere person of a King, it was a complete change of the constitution . . ." Shelburne is significantly absent from this cartoon. Above, pp. 27, 78.

3. *The State Tinkers*. Gillray. (5635) In face of national misfortunes, George III is here shown as foolishly passive: in fact, the passivity of North was forcing him to be constantly active. Above, pp. 33-4, 43.

4. *A Transfer Of East India Stock*. Sayers. (6271) Published a few days after Fox introduced his India Bill. In his pocket is the proposed new arrangement, the "seven emperors" being the seven commissioners whom Fox had named to take over the management of the East India Company's territory. Underfoot is Dunning's resolution of 1780, "that the influence of the Crown has increased, is increasing, and ought to be diminished", which had been carried in the Commons in 1780, much to the gratification of Rockingham and Shelburne supporters: its position here suggests that government patronage, previously attacked, is now once more to be increased, with "8000 Deputy Governors, 10,000 Collectors of the Revenue" to be created. Above, p. 80.

5. *Brittannia Roused*. Rowlandson. (6403) After helping to ensure the defeat of the India Bill in the Lords, George III dismissed the

NOTES ON ILLUSTRATION   133

Fox-North coalition in December 1783. The accepted date of this cartoon is February 1784, and the suggestion here that the coalition was also rejected by public opinion has some justification: their majority in the Commons was melting away quickly as Pitt showed both the intention and the ability to maintain himself as premier. In the following month, the famous 1784 election was to underline the coalition's defeat, though here it should be added that if Britannia was on Pitt's side he was also helped by the usual government advantages caustically illustrated in no. 10, below.

6. *The New Coalition.* Author unknown. (6568) One of many cartoons to lampoon the inconsistencies in the new political alignments of the period, this was published less than a fortnight after the 1784 election, when Wilkes stood once more for re-election for Middlesex, and was faced with a contest for the first time since 1769. Now declaring support for Pitt, he had Treasury money to help him, but his supine behaviour in the House had helped diminish his reputation and he beat his Foxite opponent by only 1858 votes to 1792. In this cartoon, with his staff of liberty reversed, he is given words recalling a speech of Burke's to which allusion is also made in no. 2, above.

7. *Dun-Shaw.* Gillray. (7281) In April, 1783, Dundas had brought in an India Bill of his own which made little progress: in December he had been one of the leading speakers against Fox's Bill, attacking the influence it would give him through the "seven emperors". After Pitt's India Act was finally passed in 1784, Dundas became the predominant member of the Board of Control and remained so till 1801. His political power and patronage were often attacked: in 1787, Gillray had shown him in another cartoon (7152) monopolising the Board and handing out employments to indigent Scotsmen. Here, the inscription in Dundas's turban reads: "Charged Mr F—with a design to shift the Crown from the Monarch's to his own head. Mr D. Speech." Compare no. 4, above.

8. *The Wonderful Word-Eater, lately arrived from abroad.* Dent. (7390) On hearing of the King's illness, Fox had come rushing back from holidaying in Italy, and, about three weeks before this cartoon was published, he defended the Prince's hereditary claim to become Regent in very strong terms in the Commons: in reply, Pitt maintained that to assert any claim independent of Parliamentary consent was little less than treason to the constitution, and was said to have remarked that he would "unwhig" Fox for his indiscretion. Fox, of course, was spurred on by the certain knowledge that the Regent would ask him to form a ministry, but the King's recovery, in February 1789, disappointed his hopes.

NOTES ON ILLUSTRATION

9. *The Wine Duty—or—the triumph of Bacchus and Silenus*. Gillray. (8798) New taxes, of course, were always a particularly popular subject for cartoons, and this example was published only two days after the imposition of the duty. Pitt and Dundas were well known for their love of the bottle.

10. *The Dissolution* . . . Gillray. (8805) Published two days after the dissolution of Parliament had been announced. The subsequent election, in fact, was not particularly notable: Pitt was strong in the Commons already, and remained so afterwards. He is here shown sitting on a model of the new barracks which were then being built: they had recently been attacked in the Commons, and opposition to them reflected the widespread suspicion of anything suggesting military rule.

11. *The Giant-Factotum Amusing Himself*. Gillray. (8980) Erskine and Sheridan are lying under Pitt's left foot with Fox. After the Portland Whigs had left them for Pitt, the Foxites mustered only a few dozen votes in the Commons, and, in a gesture of despair, Fox and Grey were soon to secede from the House altogether.

12. *Le Ministre D'Etat, en Grand Costume*. Gillray. (9196) The first of a series attacking the pro-French attitudes of the Foxites and their friends, and a relatively restrained example of the many cartoons vilifying their supposed revolutionary and unpatriotic ambitions. Above, p. 82.

13. *Confederated-Coalition—or—the giants storming heaven* . . . Gillray. (10240) Published on 1 May 1804, the day after the resignation of Addington's ministry became known. In April, Pitt had thrown his weight more firmly against the ministry and had abandoned his earlier attempts to remain neutral: Addington, finding his majorities slipping down to a few dozen, was unwilling to continue in face of the talents now arrayed against him. A year before, when neither Pitt nor Fox had seemed at all eager to oust him from office, Addington had survived a censure motion by 275 votes to 34. With the fall of Addington, Pitt formed a ministry, but failed to persuade the King to accept Fox: Addington himself was later to rejoin Pitt, only to leave him again and eventually come to office with Fox in the Talents ministry of 1806. The alignments here may be contrasted with those shown in no. 14, below. Above, pp. 11, 12-13.

14. *Disciples Catching the Mantle* . . . Gillray. (10992) Pitt and Fox had both died in 1806. This cartoon was published during the ministry of Portland—he being shown, suitably enough almost out of the picture, on the far left. Eldon and Perceval (who became prime minister in 1809) are kneeling: Dundas, no longer a leading

NOTES ON ILLUSTRATION

figure, peeps between Castlereagh and Canning. In the "priests of Baal", Gillray attacks the Whigs' association with the movement for Catholic emancipation, which had provoked the dismissal of their Talents ministry by George III in 1807. In such company Addington, now Lord Sidmouth, is aptly shown upside-down: he was soon to drift back to the Pittites and, in 1812, joined the cabinet formed by Liverpool (formerly Hawkesbury). St Vincent holds Sidmouth's leg. Grattan is the conspiratorial dwarf. Above, p. 12.

15. *A Head for the Cabinet.* Williams. (15372) Liverpool had a stroke in February, 1827, and after considerable delay George IV appointed Canning as his new premier on 10 April. This cartoon was published in the same month. As expected, many ministers resigned rather than serve under their former colleague, including Peel and Eldon (Lord Chancellor). Wellington resigned not only from the cabinet, but also as Commander-in-Chief. The popularity of the appointment of Canning was reflected in many cartoons, and came as a gratifying change to George IV, who was hardly used to being identified with the *vox populi* as he is here. The press, too, wrote Peel to Wellington, was "all on one side". In the King's pocket are Canning's famous lines on Pitt, "the pilot that weathered the storm". Alongside the title, as an apt example of Canning's appeal to liberal opinion, are lines from Byron's *Age of Bronze*, published in 1823:

Yet something may remain perchance to chime
With reason, and what's stranger still, with rhyme.
Even this thy genius, Canning! may permit,
Who, bred a statesman, still wast born a wit,
And never, even in that dull House, couldst tame
To unleavened prose thine own poetic flame;
Our last, our best, our only orator,
Even I can praise thee—

SELECT BIBLIOGRAPHY

1. General Histories

Briggs, A. *The Age of Improvement*. London (Longmans) 1959. A History of England, ed. W. N. Medlicott. Covers the period 1784 to 1867.

Halevy, E. *England in 1815* and *The Liberal Awakening, 1815-30*. 2nd rev. edn., London (Benn) 1949, repr. in paperback 1961. The first two volumes of Halevy's *History of the English People in the Nineteenth Century*.

Watson, J. S. *The Reign of George III, 1760-1815*. Oxford (Clarendon Press) 1960. Vol. XII of the Oxford History of England, ed. Sir George Clark. Contains a full and critical bibliography.

2. Constitutional and Political Studies

Aspinall, A. *Politics and the Press, c. 1780-1850*. London (Home & Van Thal) 1949. Full and authoritative.

— "The Reporting and Publishing of the House of Commons' Debates, 1771-1834," in *Essays Presented to Sir Lewis Namier*, edd. R. Pares and A. J. P. Taylor, London (Macmillan) 1956.

Brock, W. R. *Lord Liverpool and Liberal Toryism, 1820 to 1827*. Cambridge (University Press) 1941, repr. London (Cass) 1967. An illuminating study.

Butterfield, H. *George III and the Historians*. London (Collins) 1957. A stimulating work which takes issue with Namier at many points.

Christie, I. R. *The End of North's Ministry, 1780-1782*. London (Macmillan) 1958.

Foord, A. S. *His Majesty's Opposition, 1714-1830*. Oxford (Clarendon Press) 1964.

— "The Waning of 'The Influence of the Crown'," repr. in *Essays in Eighteenth Century History, from the English Historical Review*, arranged by R. Mitchison, London (Longmans) 1966.

SELECT BIBLIOGRAPHY 137

FEILING, Sir Keith. *The Second Tory Party 1714-1832*. London (Macmillan) 1938.

NAMIER, Sir Lewis. *Crossroads of Power, essays on eighteenth century England*. London (Hamilton) 1962. Includes the brilliant Romanes Lecture, "Monarchy and the Party System", and affords the best introduction to Namier's work on the period.
— *The Structure of Politics at the Accession of George III*. 2nd rev. edn. London (Macmillan) 1957. First published in 1929, this famous analysis has had the greatest influence on modern studies.
— *England in the Age of the American Revolution*. 2nd edn. London (Macmillan) 1961.

PARES, R. *Limited Monarchy in Great Britain in the Eighteenth Century*. London (Routledge, for The Historical Association) 1957, repr. 1963. Pamphlet no. 35 in The Historical Association's General Series, and an admirably lucid introduction.
— *King George III and the Politicians, the Ford Lectures delivered in the University of Oxford 1951-2*. Oxford (Clarendon Press) 1953, corr. repr. 1954. An indispensable interpretation.

ROBERTS, M. *The Whig Party 1807-1812*. London (Macmillan) 1939, repr. London (Cass) 1965.

VEITCH, G. S. *The Genesis of Parliamentary Reform*. London (Constable) 1913, repr., with introd. by I. R. Christie, 1965. Remains the standard work.

3. BIOGRAPHICAL AND ALLIED STUDIES

a. *General*

BROUGHAM, Lord. *Historical Sketches of Statesmen who flourished in the time of George III*. 3 pts. London 1839-43. Strongly biassed but very lively. For Brougham himself, see A. Aspinall, *Lord Brougham and the Whig Party*, Manchester (University Press) 1927.
The Debate on the American Revolution, 1761-1783, ed. M. Beloff. 2nd edn. London (A & C Black) 1960.
The Debate on the French Revolution, 1789-1800, ed. A. Cobban. 2nd edn. London (A & C Black) 1960. This volume and the one above are from the British Political Tradition Series, and contain wide selections from contemporary speeches, letters, etc.

138   SELECT BIBLIOGRAPHY

b. *George III*

BARNES, D. G. *George III and William Pitt 1783-1806, a new interpretation based upon a study of their unpublished correspondence.* Stanford (University Press) 1939.

The Later Correspondence of George III . . ., (*I*) *1783-93*; (*II*) *1793-97*, ed. A. Aspinall. Cambridge (University Press) 1962-3.

Letters from George III to Lord Bute 1756-66, ed. R. Sedgwick. London (Macmillan) 1939. Includes an interesting essay on the King's early life and character.

LONG, J. C. *George III, a biography.* London (Macdonald) 1960. Designed for the general reader.

MACALPINE, I. and HUNTER, R. "The 'Insanity' of King George III: a classic case of porphyria," in *British Medical Journal*, 1966, I. Convincingly challenges the accepted view of historians that the royal malady was "mental" in character, and from contemporary documentation argues that it derived, not from psychological illness or hereditary madness, but from a rare metabolic disorder.

c. *John Wilkes*

CHRISTIE, I. R. *Wilkes, Wyvill and Reform, the parliamentary reform movement in British politics 1760-1785.* London (Macmillan) 1962.

POSTGATE, R. W. *That Devil Wilkes.* London (Constable) 1930, rev. edn. London (Dobson) 1956. A biography.

RUDÉ, G. F. E. *Wilkes and Liberty, a social study of 1763 to 1774* Oxford (Clarendon Press) 1962. Similar in approach to the author's essay reprinted in the present volume.

d. *Charles James Fox*

HAMMOND, J. L. Le B. *Charles James Fox, a political study.* London (Methuen) 1903.

HOBHOUSE, C. *Fox.* London (Constable) 1934, 2nd edn. 1947, repr. London (Murray) 1964.

LASCELLES, E. C. P. *The Life of Charles James Fox.* Oxford (University Press) 1936, repr. 1939.

Memorials and Correspondence of Charles James Fox, ed. Lord John Russell. 4 vols. London 1853-7. Fox's letters are characteristically frank and revealing.

SELECT BIBLIOGRAPHY

TREVELYAN, Sir George O. *The Early History of Charles James Fox.* London 1880, etc. Goes up to 1774.

e. *Henry Dundas*

FURBER, H. *Henry Dundas, first Viscount Melville, 1742-1811.* Oxford (University Press) 1931. Particularly valuable on Indian administration and Scottish management.

LOVAT-FRASER, J. A. *Henry Dundas, Viscount Melville.* Cambridge (University Press) 1916.

MATHESON, C. *The Life of Henry Dundas, first Viscount Melville, 1742-1811.* London (Constable) 1933.

f. *William Pitt*

DERRY, J. W. *William Pitt.* London (Batsford) 1962. A short life from the series Makers of Britain.

ROSE, J. H. *William Pitt and National Revival.* London (Bell) 1911. From Pitt's birth to 1791.
— *William Pitt and the Great War.* London (Bell) 1911. This and the above volume were reprinted together as *Life of William Pitt*, 1923.

STANHOPE, Earl. *Life of the Right Honourable William Pitt.* 4 vols. London 1861-2. The standard life, containing many letters.

ZIEGLER, P. *Addington, a life of Henry Addington, first Viscount Sidmouth.* London (Collins) 1965. An attractive biography, also useful on Pitt and others.

g. *George Canning*

MARSHALL, D. *The Rise of George Canning.* London (Longmans) 1938.

PETRIE, Sir Charles. *George Canning.* 2nd rev. edn. London (Eyre & Spottiswoode) 1946.

ROLO, P. J. V. *George Canning, three biographical studies.* London (Macmillan) 1965. Compact and useful.

TEMPERLEY, H. W. V. *The Foreign Policy of Canning 1822-27, England, the neo-Holy Alliance and the New World.* London (Bell) 1925. 2nd edn. with a new introduction by H. Butterfield, London (Cass) 1966.

140   SELECT BIBLIOGRAPHY

4. Cartoons

GEORGE, M. D. *English Political Caricature . . . a study of opinion and propaganda,* (*I*) *to* *1792*; (*II*) *1793-1832.* 2 vols. Oxford (Clarendon Press) 1959. A most valuable survey, with more than ninety plates in each vol.

—— *Catalogue of Political and Personal Satires, preserved in the Department of Prints and Drawings in the British Museum. Vols V to X, 1771-1827.* London (British Museum) 1935-52. A magnificent work of reference giving complete descriptions of more than ten thousand prints, and explaining their meaning and background. Mrs George adds an illuminating introduction to each volume. Vol. IV, ed. F. G. Stephens (1883), covers the period 1761-70.

HILL, D. *Mr Gillray the caricaturist.* London (Phaidon) 1965. A valuable biography, with more than a hundred excellent reproductions.